1-2-3 MAGIC WORKBOOK

PRAISE FOR *1-2-3 MAGIC*

What parents are saying:

"This book **changed our lives**."

"My three-year-old has become a different little girl, **and she is so much happier now**."

"**The ideas in this book work!** It really is like magic! I feel like **I am back in charge**."

"Simple, clear, concise, and **easy to follow**."

"**I highly recommend this book** if you need a method of dealing with your little one(s) that keeps everyone calm."

"Extremely **helpful and informative**."

"A **great book** for any parent!"

"**I was desperate for a change** in my family dynamics. **This book was the answer!**"

"**Fantastic book** that really helps with toddler tantrums. **My husband and I both read it**, and now **we are disciplining in the same way**. This book has been a **lifesaver!**"

"*1-2-3 Magic* **simplifies everything** I've read in other books, which makes it **very easy to follow**. Our home has become **a much more positive place**."

"**Easy to read** and easy to follow."

"**Buy this book; read this book; follow the instructions in this book!** I highly recommend this to anyone involved in disciplining children."

"*1-2-3 Magic* **made parenting fun again**."

"All I have to say is that **the ideas in this book WORK!** It really is like magic!"

"**This book is amazing!** My three-year-old was having major tantrums four to six times a day, screaming at the top of his lungs. After applying *1-2-3 Magic*, he rarely has meltdowns."

"*1-2-3 Magic* **takes the stress out of discipline**."

"**It's such a relief to not feel like I'm constantly yelling at someone!** If you want to see a fast improvement in your child's behavior, check out *1-2-3 Magic*."

"Fantastic book that **really helps with my toddler's tantrums**."

"This is the **one-stop, go-to book** that we have referred to time and again."

"This book is a great tool! It **helped me feel confident and proud of my parenting skills**."

"The methods are described clearly, and they are **easy for any parent to follow**. I am **already seeing an improvement** in the way I react to my five- and seven-year-olds."

"We feel **more in charge** and **in control**."

"**Saved my blood pressure** and my relationship with my kids."

"**This book isn't just about time-outs and discipline**; it encompasses an entire parenting philosophy."

"**I highly recommend this book** to any parent who is **spending more time yelling at or nagging** their children **than smiling at and laughing with them**."

"**Thank you**, Dr. Phelan, for **sharing the results of your extensive research** and experimentation with the rest of the world!"

"*1-2-3 Magic* **saved my marriage**."

"This is a **must-read** for all parents."

"Our little girl had gotten full blown into the terrible twos, and **I was desperate to get the calm back in my household.** She caught on to this method in one day. **Our house is a pleasant place to be again.**"

"This book **really helps!**"

"If you have challenges with your kids and you consistently follow the directions in this book, **you will have such a better relationship with your children.**"

"I have read many discipline books and tried many different methods. **This was the one that worked for our family.**"

"Thank you, Dr. Phelan! **You are a lifesaver!**"

What experts are saying:

"**This book is easy to read and navigate.** As an in-home therapist, I need lots of parent-friendly tools to use with families, and this is one of them. **I highly recommend it!**"

"As a parent and a school social worker, **I highly recommend this book**/system to everyone."

"**A wonderful book to use with parents in therapy** to assist with parenting skills."

"As a school guidance counselor, **I highly recommend this book** to both parents and teachers."

"Great book! **I am a pediatrician, and I recommend it to my patients.**"

"**I've recommended this book for years** in my practice as a psychotherapist."

"**This is a staple** in my child therapy practice's pantry of goods."

1-2-3 MAGIC WORKBOOK

An Interactive Parenting Resource

THOMAS W. PHELAN, PhD,
AND TRACY M. LEE

to Mrs. Wilson

Copyright © 2017 by ParentMagic, Inc.
Cover and internal design © 2017 by Sourcebooks, Inc.
Cover design by Erin Seaward-Hiatt
Cover image © Blend Images, Ariel Skelley/Getty Images

This publication is designed to provide accurate and authoritative information in regard to the subject matter covered. It is sold with the understanding that the publisher is not engaged in rendering legal, accounting, or other professional service. If legal advice or other expert assistance is required, the services of a competent professional person should be sought.—*From a Declaration of Principles Jointly Adopted by a Committee of the American Bar Association and a Committee of Publishers and Associations*

Any resemblance between persons described in this book and actual persons, living or dead, is unintentional. This book is not intended to replace appropriate diagnosis and/or treatment by a qualified mental health professional or physician.

Published by Sourcebooks, Inc.
P.O. Box 4410, Naperville, Illinois 60567-4410
(630) 961-3900
Fax: (630) 961-2168
www.sourcebooks.com

Originally published in 2011 by ParentMagic, Inc.

Library of Congress Cataloging-in-Publication data is on file with the publisher.

Printed and bound in the United States of America.
VP 10 9 8 7 6 5 4 3 2 1

CONTENTS

PREFACE

MILLIONS OF PARENTS WORLDWIDE have used *1-2-3 Magic* to help them build stronger, happier families, and it seems that they are always finding new ways to use the program and make it work for their situation. The *1-2-3 Magic Workbook* helps parents better use *1-2-3 Magic* by taking them through the program chapter by chapter in order to **maximize understanding** of the material, **encourage productive self-evaluation**, and **promote the effective planning and execution** of 1-2-3 Magic parenting strategies and interventions.

One of the chief objectives of all our 1-2-3 Magic materials has always been simplicity, and that objective was especially critical in producing this workbook. You will find the *1-2-3 Magic Workbook* to be user-friendly—**simple and easy to follow** but still thought-provoking and interesting. If *1-2-3 Magic* is America's simplest parenting program, the *1-2-3 Magic Workbook* is surely America's simplest, most useful parenting workbook.

Who Can Use the New *1-2-3 Magic Workbook?*

Parents (including foster and adoptive) and other direct caretakers (grandparents, teachers, preschool, and after-school staffs) can use the *1-2-3 Magic Workbook* to improve their disciplinary effectiveness and adult-child relationship skills. After watching the *1-2-3 Magic* DVDs, listening to the CDs, or reading the book, some parents will want to work their way through the entire workbook, chapter by chapter. They can then begin to apply each new skill to their specific situation.

Mental health professionals, pediatricians, and other auxiliary staff can also use the workbook to guide the training of parents in 1-2-3 Magic. Once again, after engaging with the DVDs, CDs, or book, some folks might want to go right through the entire workbook to make absolutely sure they're doing things right. Others might decide they only need certain parts of the workbook; they might review those parts when they are having particular difficulties. For example, those struggling with testing and manipulation might want to do chapter 10—from beginning to end—before they go back to try their new methods again with their children.

The *1-2-3 Magic Workbook* can be used as a **training guide for one-on-one clinical sessions** with individual families, but it can also serve as a structure for one- to two-hour group therapy-training sessions with multiple families. Chapter sections such as "Questions for Reflection/Discussion," "What Would You Suggest?" "How Are Things at Your House?" "Putting 1-2-3 Magic into Action with Your Family," and "Troubleshooting Exercises" provide an excellent basis for productive and provocative group discussions.

How to Use This Book

The *1-2-3 Magic Workbook* has two main sections. In **parts I through IV, we examine each chapter of** *1-2-3 Magic*, breaking the treatment of the material down into seven parts:

1. Overview of Content
2. Questions for Reflection/Discussion
3. Case Study
4. "What Would You Suggest?" Solutions for the Case Study
5. "How Are Things at Your House?" Self-Evaluation
6. Putting 1-2-3 Magic into Action with Your Family
7. Troubleshooting Exercises
8. Chapter Summary

In the Stories and Questions section, we present illustrated, comic-type stories that show how real parents actually applied 1-2-3 Magic strategies when faced with challenges from their children. The true stories are entertaining and engaging, and they include further questions for reflection and discussion.

Whether you are a parent, a mental health professional, or both, we hope the *1-2-3 Magic Workbook* provides you with valuable assistance in applying **America's most popular child discipline program.**

That young mother would be me. And this wasn't any fairy tale.

MY NAME'S LISA. LET'S START WITH MY STORY. SINGLE MOTHER OF THREE LIVING IN PITTSBURGH.

Brandon, 11, Katie, 9, and Josh, 5, were cute as buttons. But they were driving me nuts!

They fought like cats and dogs. So I would yell.

KNOCK IT OFF!!!!

They wouldn't go to bed on time. So I would scream.

GO TO BED!!!

They would tantrum till I gave them their way.

OK, OK!! HERE!

And they were making a mess of my whole house.

My ex claimed he had no problems with them—on weekends!

I was depressed. I loved my kids but I didn't like them at all.

So I read huge books about parenting.

But in the heat of the battle, I couldn't remember what I was supposed to do.

Some parents suggested spanking, but I didn't like that idea.

Other parents told me I needed to explain more, but the kids didn't seem to care what I said.

I felt like I was drowning.

Then one day an old high school friend flew in for my birthday. She would soon be the best birthday gift I ever got.

After Sally saw what was happening at my house, she told me her story.

Several years back, her two kids had been running **her** house.

Then she and her husband came across a parenting program with a strange name.

IT WAS CALLED *1-2-3 MAGIC*. WE GOT THE BOOK AND DVD.

⁉

The program was simple and easy to learn. They mastered it in just a few hours.

LOOK AT THIS!

YEP, THAT'S US.

Sally told me the story of how she and her husband then sat their kids down and explained that things were going to be different.

THE KIDS, OF COURSE, DIDN'T BELIEVE US.

She told me how they shaped up fighting, bedtime, whining, and homework.

IT TOOK LESS THAN 10 DAYS TO MAKE BELIEVERS OUT OF THEM.

Sally's stories gave me a sense of optimism I had never had before. I got the *1-2-3 Magic* book and DVD on the web.

The next day I was ready. The kids never knew what hit them! For fighting I used counting.

THAT'S 1 FOR BOTH OF YOU.

For bedtime I used the Basic Bedtime Method and the kitchen timer.

I'M SETTING THE TIMER FOR 30 MINUTES.

For tantrums and disrespect I used counting again.

THAT'S 3, TAKE 5.

And for picking up I used the timer, the Garbage Bag method, and lots of praise.

8 O'CLOCK GUYS. ANYTHING OUT GOES IN THE BAG.

MOM!

I worked hard—and I worked my kids even harder. They didn't like me very much for a while.

BUT FOR ONCE I KNEW EXACTLY WHAT I WAS DOING!

Pretty soon I was actually enjoying my children again. They were really a pretty nice bunch!

My house became more peaceful and quiet. I didn't dread coming home from work all the time.

One day Brandon shocked me. He said he liked 1-2-3 Magic. What!? I asked why.

BECAUSE YOU DON'T YELL SO MUCH ANYMORE.

In just a few weeks I had gone a long way toward being the kind of parent I wanted to be.

Questions for You

I felt like I was drowning.

Do you ever feel like this as a parent?

1	2	3	4	5
Never	Seldom	Sometimes	Often	Always

What is going on when your home is out of control?

_____

_____

_____

How does this make you feel about yourself?

_____

_____

_____

Friendly Advice?

Did Lisa need to "crack down"?

_____

_____

_____

Does cracking down have to mean physical discipline?

_____

_____

_____

Friendly Advice?

Are explanations helpful with your kids in discipline situations?

_____

_____

_____

When do you think explanations are absolutely necessary?

_____

_____

_____

Attitude Adjustment Part 1: The Kids

How did Lisa's son feel at this point about the transformation in his mother? Did he cooperate willingly with the change?

_____

_____

How did the boy feel at the end? _____

_____

Attitude Adjustment Part 2: The Parent

List three major factors that caused the change in Lisa's attitude.

1. _____

   _____

2. _____

   _____

3. _____

   _____

You too can take control of your home, start enjoying your children, and be the kind of parent you want to be. **And today it is the perfect day to begin!**

You too can take control of your home, start enjoying your children, and be the kind of parent you want to be. **All in the very near future!**

PART I

Building a Solid Foundation for Parenting

1

ORIENTATION TO THE PARENTING PROFESSION

How to Prepare for the World's Most Important Job

Chapter Overview

Children do not enter the world with instructions, but after the initial excitement of bringing your new baby home, you may begin wishing kids did have a How-to-Raise-Me manual. In this chapter, you will learn some of the basics you will need to raise happy, confident, and independent kids. You will learn how to begin with the right perspective and how to examine your automatic parenting responses. In addition, you will find out what to expect when you begin using 1-2-3 Magic with your children.

Questions about Chapter 1

1. What are the two most important qualities of effective parents?
2. When is your automatic response to your child a good thing?

3. When should you replace an automatic response with a strategy learned from 1-2-3 Magic?

4. How should you start the 1-2-3 Magic program?

5. What are the two possible responses from your child when you begin using 1-2-3 Magic?

Key Concept

Research has shown that effective parents are warm and friendly on the one hand, but also demanding and firm on the other. Both orientations are critical to raising emotionally intelligent and mature kids.

Case Study

Jill loves her kids, eight-year-old Michael and four-year-old Kennedy. Jill loves to read to them before bed and play board games with them. However, lately Jill has been having some trouble with her kids. Michael teases Kennedy nonstop, and going to the store with both of them leads to tantrums and sibling rivalry. Jill and her husband have talked with Michael about how he should treat his sister, but Michael continues to aggravate Kennedy. The store issue is not getting any better. The past few times they've had to go to the store, Jill has just bought the kids candy and toys to keep them quiet.

WHAT WOULD YOU SUGGEST?

1. Based on the information in chapter 1, what is Jill doing right?

_____

_____

_____

2. Where can Jill improve?

_____

_____

_____

How Are Things at Your House?

Rate yourself on a scale of 1 to 5 in the following parenting areas. 1 means **not so good**, and 5 means **fantastic**.

NOT SO GOOD ·· FANTASTIC

1   2   3   4   5

Warm and Friendly_____   Positive Automatic Responses_____

Demanding and Firm_____   Negative Automatic Responses_____

Putting 1-2-3 Magic into Action with Your Family

Now it's time to start putting what you've learned so far into action. Here are some questions and exercises to help you begin making plans for dealing with your children.

1. Which negative automatic responses do you need to replace with more deliberate, respectful actions?

   _____

   _____

   _____

2. Think about your children and their personalities. Do you think they will be "immediate cooperators" or "immediate testers"?

   _____

   _____

   _____

Troubleshooting Exercise

Automatic responses are tough to change because they are, well…automatic. Think about the times when you have had some negative automatic responses as a parent. Describe some of them here and take note of when they happened. Knowing when you are likely to have a negative automatic response to your children will be helpful when you begin to replace these negative times with a more positive parental approach.

_____

_____

_____

_____

CHAPTER SUMMARY

1. Parents should be both warm/friendly and demanding/firm.
2. Positive automatic parenting habits should be maintained.
3. Negative parenting habits should be replaced with deliberate and respectful strategies.
4. Kids will fall into either the "immediate cooperator" or "immediate tester" category once the 1-2-3 Magic plan is implemented.

2

YOUR JOB AS A PARENT

Three Things You Can Do to Raise Happy, Healthy Kids

Chapter Overview

Parenting can be an overwhelming task. Dealing with whining and tantrums, helping with homework, and getting kids to bed are just a few of the many tasks to be done. This chapter will simplify the work of parenting into three basic jobs. The first job involves controlling obnoxious behavior. In this step you will learn to **Stop** negative behavior like screaming and whining. Job 2 involves encouraging good behavior. We call this **Start** behavior since it deals with getting your child to do things like homework and room cleaning. The last important job focuses on **strengthening your relationship** with your child.

Questions about Chapter 2

1. What are the three parenting jobs?
2. What is the difference between Stop and Start behavior?
3. What are some examples of Stop and Start behavior?

4. Which kind of behavior requires more motivation, Stop or Start?

5. What are some benefits of strengthening your bond with your kids?

Case Study

Mary is very frustrated and having a difficult time with her eight-year-old son, John. Every evening has turned into a battle. When Mary tells John it's time to start his homework, an argument occurs. John yells and throws a tantrum. Mary usually gets upset too. In addition, John is continually making his younger sister, Abby, cry by saying mean things to her. Mary loves John but is just tired and worn out from John's problem behavior at night. She desperately would like more peaceful evenings with her children.

WHAT WOULD YOU SUGGEST?

1. Identify the Stop behavior and the Start behavior problems that Mary needs to deal with.

_____

_____

2. According to the information in this chapter, which strategies should Mary use to address Stop behavior and which strategies should she use for Start behavior?

_____

_____

Quick Tip

Exactly how you start depends on how much energy you have. If you feel like you're barely hanging on by your fingernails, you might want to start with only counting. Then add the good behavior and relationship steps after the kids know you mean business.

How Are Things at Your House?

Rate yourself on a scale of 1 to 5 in the following parenting areas.

| NOT SO GOOD ·································· FANTASTIC |
| 1   2   3   4   5 |

How are you doing currently with Stop behaviors (screaming, whining, tantrums, and so on)? _____

How are you doing with Start behaviors (going to bed, homework, getting up in the morning, and so on)? _____

Putting 1-2-3 Magic into Action with Your Family

1. Remember that Stop behaviors are those actions your child does that you want him or her to stop doing (such as whining or complaining). Make a list of Stop behaviors you would like to address with your child. If you have more than one child, make a list for each.

   _____

   _____

   _____

   _____

2. Remember that Start behaviors are those actions you would like your child to begin doing (such as doing homework or going to bed). Make a list of those Start behaviors you would like to see your child begin without a fight. If you have more than one child, make a list for each.

   _____

   _____

   _____

   _____

Troubleshooting Exercise

Since counting is so easy, one of the biggest problems we encounter is parents attempting to use counting for Start behavior. In the list of behaviors below, check the Stop behaviors that you should count when they occur.

- ❏ Cleaning rooms
- ❏ Arguing with a sibling
- ❏ Not eating vegetables
- ❏ Whining in the car
- ❏ Begging for candy at the store
- ❏ Going to bed on time
- ❏ Not practicing a musical instrument
- ❏ Throwing a football in the house
- ❏ Refusing to come inside when asked
- ❏ Leaving shoes all over the house

CHAPTER SUMMARY

1. There are three basic jobs of parenting: controlling obnoxious behavior, encouraging good behavior, and strengthening your relationship with your child.
2. Counting is to be used for Stop behavior.
3. Encouraging good behavior requires you to use tactics that will encourage more motivation in your kids.
4. A good relationship with your child makes parenting easier and more fun.

3

CHALLENGING THE LITTLE ADULT ASSUMPTION

Why You Need to Remember That Kids Are Just Kids

Chapter Overview

Many parents carry around in their heads an enchanting but troublesome notion that causes discipline failures. This idea is known as the "Little Adult Assumption," and this assumption often causes stormy scenes that can even lead to physical child abuse. Parents with this idea rely too heavily on words and reasoning and not enough on simple techniques that children can easily understand. This chapter challenges the Little Adult Assumption and provides an alternative view of kids and parenting. In addition, you will begin to understand the overall orientation of 1-2-3 Magic as you learn about the notion of "dictatorship to democracy."

Questions about Chapter 3

1. What is the Little Adult Assumption?
2. What strategies do adults who believe the Little Adult Assumption rely on in dealing with their kids?

3. What is one big danger in relying heavily on words and reasoning for disciplining children?

4. What does "dictatorship to democracy" mean?

5. What is one fear many parents have that can negatively affect their parenting?

Case Study

Tyler, Linda's six-year-old son, always wants to stay up with his older brother, Trevor, who is fifteen. Tyler's bedtime is at eight thirty, and Trevor usually goes to bed about ten. Every night when Linda tries to put Tyler to bed, he doesn't want to go. Linda usually begins by calmly explaining to Tyler why his brother gets to stay up later because he is older. Tyler usually argues with his mother, getting her upset. The conflict often escalates, with Tyler's father intervening and spanking Tyler. Linda desperately wants a calmer bedtime ritual with her son, but she doesn't know what to do.

WHAT WOULD YOU SUGGEST?

1. What are the two main parenting problems you see in the story above?

_____

_____

2. What is the first thing Linda needs to do to turn bedtime around at her house?

_____

_____

Caution

One explanation, if really necessary, is fine. It's the attempts at *repeated explanations* that get adults and kids into trouble. Too much parent talking irritates and distracts children.

How Are Things at Your House?

Rate yourself on a scale of 1 to 5 in the following parenting areas.

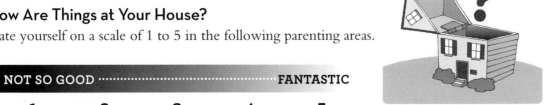

NOT SO GOOD ·································· FANTASTIC

1   2   3   4   5

Talking too much during discipline situations_____

How well is your parenting going using the Little Adult Assumption?_____

Explain.

_____

_____

_____

_____

Putting 1-2-3 Magic into Action with Your Family

1. Understanding the Little Adult Assumption is the key to understanding how to apply 1-2-3 Magic. In your own words, write a description of what the Little Adult Assumption means.

_____

_____

2. How easy will it be for you to switch from explaining to training your kids?

_____

_____

Troubleshooting Exercise

Take a moment to list those times when you are most likely to operate with the Little Adult Assumption (bedtime, at the store, after school, and so on).

_____   _____

_____   _____

_____   _____

CHAPTER SUMMARY

1. The Little Adult Assumption is the cause of most discipline mistakes.
2. Parents often rely too heavily on words and reasoning.
3. Parents should begin as benevolent dictators and gradually move toward a more democratic parenting style as their kids get older and more independent.

4

AVOIDING THE TWO BIGGEST DISCIPLINE MISTAKES

The Dangers of Too Much Talking and Too Much Emotion

Chapter Overview

The two biggest mistakes that parents make in dealing with children are these: **Too Much Talking** and **Too Much Emotion**. While too much talking can irritate and distract kids, too much emotion can be even more destructive. It can result in adult outbursts and actions that parents ultimately regret. When it comes to discipline, you want to be consistent, decisive, and calm. This chapter analyzes why kids sometimes seem to want to upset their parents, and how parents can keep themselves quiet and under control in these situations.

Questions about Chapter 4

1. Why does Too Much Talking make kids less likely to cooperate?
2. What is a possible reward for a child if he gets his parents upset?
3. What are three important guidelines for discipline?

4. What are the two important rules in applying the 1-2-3 Magic plan?

5. What are some ways that some parents remind themselves about the No Talking and No Emotion Rules?

Case Study

Amy's two-year-old son, Matthew, whines all the time. No matter how much attention Amy gives Matthew, he continues whining when he wants something. Amy has told him over and over not to whine. She's also tried giving Matthew extra attention. Nothing seems to work. Lately, she's been getting upset and yelling at him because she is so frustrated. Amy feels guilty about her explosions, but she just doesn't know what to do.

WHAT WOULD YOU SUGGEST?

1. Based on the information in chapter 4, what are some of the parenting problems you see in the story above?

_____

_____

2. What is the first thing Amy needs to realize?

_____

_____

_____

Quick Tip

If your little child can get big old you all upset, your upset is the big splash for him. Your emotional outburst accidentally makes your child feel powerful.

How Are Things at Your House?

Rate yourself on a scale of 1 to 5 in the following parenting areas.

NOT SO GOOD ··· FANTASTIC

1   2   3   4   5

Talking too much _____
Getting too upset _____

If you rated yourself below a 5, what are some ways you can improve?

_____

_____

Putting 1-2-3 Magic into Action with Your Family

1. How can you show more positive feedback, such as affection and praise, to your child?

   _____

   _____

   _____

2. What are some ways your child gets you upset? How will you counteract his attempts in the future?

   _____

   _____

   _____

Troubleshooting Exercise

Following the No Talking and No Emotion Rules can be challenging for some parents. In the heat of the moment, how will you remind yourself not to talk or get upset?

_____

_____

_____

_____

CHAPTER SUMMARY

1. Express your emotion toward your child when it is positive.
2. Too much talking interferes with discipline.
3. Too much emotion can lead to adult emotional outbursts and can reinforce bad behavior.

Too Much Talking
Too Much Emotion

PART II

Controlling Obnoxious Behavior

Parenting Job 1

CHAPTER 5
Getting Results through Counting

CHAPTER 6
Advice for Nearly Any Counting Challenge

CHAPTER 7
Disciplining Your Child in Public

CHAPTER 8
How to Handle Sibling Rivalry,
Tantrums, Pouting, and Lying

CHAPTER 9
Getting Started with Counting

5

GETTING RESULTS THROUGH COUNTING

Sometimes Your Silence Speaks Louder Than Your Words

Chapter Overview

This chapter will show you the nuts and bolts of controlling obnoxious behavior in your kids. The 1-2-3 method will help you regain control, and it will help your kids take more responsibility for their own behavior. This method will not be difficult for you to learn. It is straightforward and easy for both you and your children to understand. The part that can be a little tough is remembering to keep away from the two big parenting mistakes—too much talking and too much emotion!

Remember: Excessive parental chattering and emotional outbursts will ruin any discipline program!

Questions about Chapter 5

1. Why is the 1-2-3 method "simple but not always easy"?
2. How long should you wait between counts?

3. What happens after your child comes out of time-out?
4. What is an example of an "automatic 3"?
5. Give some examples of time-out alternatives.

Case Study

Tom's daughter, Tina, has thrown a huge temper tantrum because she wanted to go outside and play after her father had told her that it was time to do her homework. Tom told her no, and the screaming and badgering began. Tom counted Tina, got to three, and sent her to time-out for seven minutes. Tom was furious at her for having been so difficult to deal with. Now the seven-minute time-out is over, and Tina comes out of her room and goes directly to her father for a hug. Tom is still angry with her and wants to sit her down and tell her how things are going to be from now on.

WHAT WOULD YOU SUGGEST?

1. Is Tom on the right track? Should he speak to Tina about her behavior right after she has completed her time-out?

_____

_____

_____

2. Give an example of an appropriate way that you would interact with Tina after her time-out. What would you say to her?

_____

_____

_____

How Are Things at Your House?

1. Think about the primary disciplinarians in your child's life. Which adult is the most likely to have trouble with the No Talking Rule?

_____

_____

2. Which adult will have the most trouble with the No Emotion Rule?

_____

_____

Putting 1-2-3 Magic into Action with Your Family

Think of your children one at a time. Given what you know about them, who is probably going to have the most trouble handling the new law of the land? If you only have one child, what do you think he or she will have the most trouble handling on the new program?

_____

_____

_____

_____

Key Concept
When you talk too much, you switch your child's focus off the need for good behavior and on to the possibility of an enjoyable argument.

Troubleshooting Exercise

There may be times when your children decide to be very stubborn and not willingly go to their time-out areas. For each of your children, make a list of three time-out alternatives that you could use. The list may be the same or different for each of your children.

_____   _____

_____   _____

_____   _____

CHAPTER SUMMARY

There are several benefits to counting. Less stress for you, short punishments for your kids, and more time for fun for everyone!

The No Talking and No Emotion Rules are vital to the success of the counting method.

6

ADVICE FOR NEARLY ANY COUNTING CHALLENGE

Answers to Our Most Frequently Asked Questions

Chapter Overview

This chapter is full of answers to many questions that parents have regarding how to apply the 1-2-3 method. By this time, in fact, you have probably thought of at least a half-dozen of these questions yourself! Read chapter 6 carefully and apply the principles. This preparation will help you to not be caught by surprise every time your children do not cooperate perfectly. You will soon see improved behavior from your kids, and you will be able to enjoy them a lot more!

Questions about Chapter 6

1. What are some challenges that may present themselves when you try to use a time-out chair instead of a room?
2. What kind of disciplinarians do your children's grandparents tend to be?

3. How do you apply the 1-2-3 method when you're on the phone?
4. What should you do if your child doesn't want to come out of a time-out when his or her time is up?
5. Does being counted affect a child's self-esteem in a positive or negative way?

Case Study

Jack's four-year-old son, Ethan, can be quite a handful. Ethan becomes very upset when he gets counted and the count reaches 3. Today, Ethan is attempting to grab a toy from his older brother. Jack counts him in an attempt to get him to let go of the toy. Ethan does not let go and gets to a count of 3. He does not go to his room voluntarily, so Jack has to carry him there. Now Ethan is coming out repeatedly and refusing to stay put for his time-out.

WHAT WOULD YOU SUGGEST?

1. List three things that Jack can do to ensure that Ethan stays in his room.

_____

_____

_____

2. Which of these three methods would you choose to try first?

_____

How Are Things at Your House?

1. Before you start 1-2-3 Magic, what concepts do you feel need to be clarified?

   _____

   _____

2. How does counting compare to what you are currently doing to manage your children?

   _____

   _____

3. What aspects of counting are you uncomfortable with (if any)?

   _____

Putting 1-2-3 Magic into Action with Your Family

1. Sometimes grandparents do not cooperate with your discipline plans for your children. How will you handle this situation if it arises?

   _____

   _____

2. How will you handle the issue of whether or not to make your kids apologize for their transgressions?

   _____

   _____

Key Concept

The point behind 1-2-3 Magic is that parents are ready for anything, rather than worrying what the kids are going to do next. The message is: "I love you and it's my job to train and discipline you. I don't expect you to be perfect, and when you act up, this is what I will do."

Troubleshooting Exercise

Before you begin using 1-2-3 Magic, go through chapter 6 very carefully and find the difficult issues that you think may apply to each of your children. List the issues below. Creating a plan prior to needing one will help you tremendously.

_____

_____

_____

_____

_____

_____

Keep in mind that every child is different. Some children react beautifully to starting the 1-2-3 method of discipline, while others do a lot of testing to see if you will stick with the program. Respect your child's individuality and find the solutions that work for your family.

CHAPTER SUMMARY

Most common situations related to the 1-2-3 discipline plan have easy solutions.

Keep the book handy so you can refer to it often.

7

DISCIPLINING YOUR CHILD IN PUBLIC

How to Handle Grocery Store Meltdowns and Other Embarrassing Situations

Chapter Overview

Being out in public presents its own parenting challenges. When our kids choose to challenge us out there in the big, bad world, we sometimes have to deal with our own red-hot embarrassment, which causes us to become far more frazzled than we would be at home. Additionally, we have to contend with logistical issues involving the time-out. Chapter 7 deals with these situations. If we can formulate a plan before these circumstances arise, it makes it easier to handle them when they occur.

Questions about Chapter 7

1. What is so difficult about handling challenging behavior in public?
2. What are some examples of time-out places that you can use in public?
3. Why do you give four counts with the "1-2-3-4"?

4. How can you handle difficult behavior in the car?

5. What is the most important thing to remember about long car trips?

Case Study

Jan is walking through the grocery store with her three-year-old son, Billy. They enter the snack aisle, and Billy immediately hones in on the chocolate chip cookies. He attempts to grab them from the shelf, and Jan tells him to stop. He looks at his mother, digs in his heels, and yells, "But I WANT the cookies!" Again, Jan tells Billy that he can't have the cookies, but that she will be happy to give him the crackers that she brought from home instead. Billy throws himself onto the floor, right there in aisle five, and screams as though someone were assaulting him.

WHAT WOULD YOU SUGGEST?

1. Identify the Stop behavior that Billy is presenting.

_____

_____

2. What specific first step should Jan take to stop this behavior?

_____

_____

3. Name one time-out spot that Jan could use in this situation.

_____

_____

Quick Tip

When you're out in public, there is always a room, something like a room, or a symbolic location where a time-out can be served. And don't forget your time-out alternatives. Just because people are watching does not mean that you have to be at your kids' mercy!

How Are Things at Your House?

On a scale from 1 to 5 (with 1 meaning that your child's behavior in public is generally AWFUL and 5 meaning there are NO PROBLEMS), rate the behavior of each of your children.

AWFUL ·· NO PROBLEMS

1   2   3   4   5

Rate _____ Rate _____ Rate _____ Rate _____

1. How does your child generally behave in public? (If you have more than one child, do this for each one.)

   _____

   _____

   _____

2. Repeat the exercise for your child's behavior during car trips.

   _____

   _____

   _____

Putting 1-2-3 Magic into Action with Your Family

1. Using what you learned in chapter 7, describe how you will now handle temper tantrums in public.

_____

2. How will you handle misbehavior in the car?

_____

Troubleshooting Exercises

1. Put on your thinking cap before you go out into the world with your kids! Write down three things that you can do to make your time in public easier and more fun for you and your children.

_____

2. How have you handled problem behavior in public with your children in the past? Have your methods been effective?

_____

CHAPTER SUMMARY

1. **Remember that time-out doesn't have to occur in your child's room.** Be creative, and you can probably come up with a suitable time-out spot when you are out and about.
2. **Fight your mortification at your child's public temper tantrums.** All parents have been there, and most have nothing but sympathy for your difficult moment. The people who haven't been there don't understand anyway, so don't worry about what they think!

8

HOW TO HANDLE SIBLING RIVALRY, TANTRUMS, POUTING, AND LYING

Managing Four Common Behavioral Problems

Chapter Overview

Some situations require minor modifications of the 1-2-3 Magic program. What do you do when your kids are fighting and you have no idea who the main culprit is? What do you do when the time-out period is over, but your daughter is still throwing a major tantrum in her room? And what about pouting? Your son isn't really making any noise, but he's definitely trying to push your buttons with his whole "woe is me" routine! Sibling rivalry, tantrums, pouting, and lying are covered in this chapter.

Questions about Chapter 8

1. When your children are fighting, how do you know who gets counted?
2. What are the two ridiculous questions that a parent should never ask fighting children?
3. What should you do if both fighting children share a room and they receive a count of 3?

4. What happens if you send a child to time-out and her tantrum continues?
5. How should a parent handle pouting?
6. When you suspect a child is lying, why is it important not to corner the child?

Case Study

Theresa's daughter, Jennifer, was angry because she didn't get to play her favorite electronic game before bedtime. She was feeling very sorry for herself, sitting on the couch with her arms crossed and a pouty look on her face. Theresa was mildly amused but didn't show it. She walked into the kitchen. Jennifer decided to follow. What good is being upset if there is no one around to notice it? What Theresa had thought was a little funny a few minutes before was now becoming quite irritating. Being followed around by an actively unhappy child was not funny at all!

WHAT WOULD YOU SUGGEST?

1. Is Jennifer engaging in regular pouting or aggressive pouting?

_____

2. If you were Theresa, how would you handle this situation?

_____

_____

_____

Caution

Never ask the world's two stupidest questions, "Who started it?" and "What happened?" unless you think someone is physically injured. Do you expect your kids to come up with George Washington's version of "I cannot tell a lie"?

How Are Things at Your House?

1. Think of all your children. Does one of your children tend to bully the others? Perhaps you have a child who is a perpetual victim (in his own mind!) and a bit of a tattletale. Discuss how either of these dynamics might come into play and how you would manage them.

_____

_____

_____

2. Did you have siblings? Compare your relationships with your siblings to your children's relationships with theirs. Remembering that you were once where your kids are now can help you handle your emotional reaction to sibling rivalry.

_____

_____

_____

Putting 1-2-3 Magic into Action with Your Family

1. Using what you learned in chapter 8, describe what you will do differently when dealing with sibling rivalry.

_____

_____

_____

2. If your children share a room, make a short list of alternative time-out locations for one of them to use in the event of a time-out for both of them due to fighting.

_____   _____

_____   _____

_____   _____

Troubleshooting Exercise

Your child is passively pouting, and it's getting on your nerves. What can you do, since counting isn't recommended as a first option? Thinking this out ahead of time can help you stay calm when the situation arises.

_____

_____

_____

CHAPTER SUMMARY

1. Remember that nothing you do will put a permanent end to sibling rivalry. Live with it and manage it as best you can.
2. Pouting is ignored unless the child becomes an aggressive pouter.
3. With kids four and older, time-out doesn't start until the temper tantrum ends!

Remember to avoid cornering your kids if you suspect they are lying to you.

9
GETTING STARTED WITH COUNTING

How to Talk to Your Kids about
1-2-3 Magic and the New House Rules

Chapter Overview

Congratulations! You are ready to begin the 1-2-3 Magic program in earnest. Do you just start throwing numbers around and hope for the best? No! Now it's time to let your precious progeny in on what's about to happen in all your lives. What you need to do is to have a short conversation with your kids explaining the nuts and bolts of counting. More importantly, let them know how it is going to improve all your lives immeasurably. Won't they be surprised! One great resource to use for this conversation is *1-2-3 Magic for Kids*, an easy-to-understand illustrated storybook that explains the program from a kid's point of view.

Questions about Chapter 9

1. About how long should the Kickoff Conversation last?
2. What is the best way to handle this conversation for parents who live apart?

3. What part of the 1-2-3 program do you tell your kids that they will actually like?
4. Do you think your kids will believe you are serious?
5. How will you manage any questions your kids have?

Case Study

Jim and Michelle decide to sit their children down and tell them about 1-2-3 Magic. Their twelve-year-old daughter, Taylor, responds with sarcastic laughter, and their ten-year-old son, John, responds with "This is so stupid!"

WHAT WOULD YOU SUGGEST?

If you are Jim and Michelle, how do you respond to your kids' attitudes?

_____

_____

_____

How Are Things at Your House?

Do either you or your partner have trouble with the No Talking Rule? If so, be aware of this. Use the lines below to come up with a short and sweet start to your Kickoff Conversation.

_____

_____

_____

_____

Putting 1-2-3 Magic into Action with Your Family

1. If you have a child who is two or three years old, how can you explain the 1-2-3 method to her?

_____

_____

2. How will you explain counting to a ten-year-old?

_____

_____

Quick Tip

It's very important to rehearse or role-play the counting procedure for little kids as well as older children. This gives the children a real feel for what's going to happen, and it also lets them know you're serious about making some changes at home.

Troubleshooting Exercise

Remember that your kids will probably not jump up and hug you for deciding to bring 1-2-3 Magic into their lives. Keep your expectations realistic, and when in doubt, count.

What will you do if your nine-year-old son says, "This is dumb and all our friends think you guys are weird!"?

_____

_____

_____

CHAPTER SUMMARY

You've learned the 1-2-3 method, you've had most of your questions answered, and you alerted your offspring to what lies ahead. Now it's time to get started!

**You're almost ready to begin your first
giant parenting step:**

Controlling Obnoxious Behavior!

PART III

Managing Testing and Manipulation

10

RECOGNIZING THE SIX TYPES OF TESTING AND MANIPULATION

How to Prepare for Kids Resisting 1-2-3 Magic

Chapter Overview

When you begin 1-2-3 Magic, there are actually some children who will be immediate cooperators. They will understand the new rules quickly and will comply with the time-outs that you give. In fact, these are the kids who will rarely get to a count of three. Our guess is that the immediate cooperator in your house, if there is one, isn't the reason that you purchased this book! There is probably another child (or two!) who is not going to be happy with all this new stuff that you're introducing. Welcome to testing and manipulation!

Questions about Chapter 10

1. List the Six Kinds of Testing and Manipulation.
2. What is the one kind of testing and manipulation that does *not* get counted?
3. Why is it bad if your child has a favorite tactic?

4. What is the easiest but worst way to get a child to stop testing and manipulating?

5. What is a 4-1 testing pattern?

Case Study

The Lopez family had a Kickoff Conversation with their kids two days ago. Today, their eleven-year-old-son, Juan, asks his father, Marc, if he can spend the night with a friend. It's a Tuesday in February. Marc tells Juan that he can't spend the night with his friend because they have a rule about not having sleepovers on school nights. Juan becomes very angry. He picks up a book that is sitting on his dad's desk and forcefully throws it to the floor.

WHAT WOULD YOU SUGGEST?

1. Identify the testing tactic that Juan is using in the scenario above.

_____

2. What is the best course of action for Marc to take with Juan right now?

_____

How Are Things at Your House?

1. Think of all your children. Currently, what is the favored testing tactic that each of your children uses?

CHILD	TACTIC
_____	_____
_____	_____
_____	_____

2. What does this mean for you and your discipline?

_____

_____

Quick Tip

A child who is testing you is offering you a deal: give me what I want, and my badgering, temper, threat, or martyrdom will stop—immediately! Does that sound like a deal you can't refuse? Think again!

Putting 1-2-3 Magic into Action with Your Family

1. What is the proper way to handle most forms of testing and manipulation?

_____

_____

2. What are the exceptions to counting testing and manipulation?

_____

_____

3. Let's say that your child tests you. You frustrate him by telling him no, and he immediately starts in with temper. "This is stupid!" You count him, but he continues this behavior and winds up in time-out. He comes out of time-out and immediately begins with a new tactic—martyrdom. He says, "You don't love me anymore!" How do you deal with round two of the testing and manipulation?

_____

_____

Troubleshooting Exercises

1. When your child begins to test you, in the beginning of the ordeal, it can be easy to keep your cool. However, some kids are masters and keep on and on and on, even after you send them to time-out! Some kids know that if they keep on long enough, they can make you break! One of the worst things you can do with testing and manipulation is to keep your cool for a long time and then lose it. Come up with a short list of things you can do to help you remain calm under these circumstances.

_____   _____

_____   _____

_____   _____

2. Keep in mind that some children will jump from tactic to tactic if one isn't working for them. As frustrating as this is, it means that you are doing well! Try to remember this, and it should help ease your frustration during the first difficult days.

_____   _____

_____   _____

CHAPTER SUMMARY

The Six Kinds of Testing and Manipulation: badgering, temper, threat, martyrdom, butter up, and physical tactics.

Keep in mind that a child who is testing is doing it out of frustration. Testing won't last forever—if you handle it correctly!

Key Concept

The first goal of testing is for the child to get what he wants. Since he's less powerful than you are, he must use some emotional manipulation. If the child still fails to get what he wants, the second goal of testing is often retaliation or revenge.

11

TALES FROM THE TRENCHES

Real Stories from Real Parents

Chapter Overview

This chapter provides some real-life scenarios involving different adults using 1-2-3 Magic. This will give you a feel for how counting should work and what some of the pitfalls may be. However, we'll also show you how to climb out of the pits you may fall into! These examples will demonstrate how we sometimes allow ourselves to get overly chatty or emotional. The examples will also demonstrate how to stay on your toes and avoid those parenting mistakes.

Questions about Chapter 11

1. In most instances, what is the best way to handle a problem between siblings?
2. What question should you never ask two fighting siblings?
3. We aren't supposed to use counting with a child who has been told to go to bed and doesn't. Why not?
4. In the "Dog Teasing" scenario in this chapter, Mom has to physically escort the child to time-out. What if your child is almost your size and refuses to go? What do you do?

5. Under the section in the chapter labeled "Constant Requests," Tom's mother added five minutes to his ten-minute time-out. Why?

Case Study

Your daughters are in their shared bedroom playing with their dolls together. Out of nowhere, you hear yelling coming from the room. Both girls are screaming at the tops of their lungs! You walk into the room and find them playing tug-of-war with a doll's dress.

WHAT WOULD YOU SUGGEST?

1. Who do you count?

_____

2. If the kids get to three, how do you handle the time-out? Remember, they share a bedroom.

_____

_____

_____

3. How should parents handle their personal frustrations with sibling rivalry?

_____

_____

_____

How Are Things at Your House?

1. What is one of the main reasons that parents have such a hard time disciplining in public?

_____

_____

2. How can you address this? Write down a few things that you can tell yourself in public that will help you to get beyond this.

_____

_____

Putting 1-2-3 Magic into Action with Your Family

1. How do you handle problems that arise with your child's behavior when he has friends over to play?

_____

_____

_____

2. Which of your children gives you the most trouble out in public? List a few ways you can prepare yourself (and your child!) before you even leave the house.

_____

_____

_____

Troubleshooting Exercises

1. It's very easy to allow our own frustrations and bad moods to affect our parenting, even when our moods have nothing at all to do with our children. Be aware of this fact and try very hard to keep a cool head when disciplining, even when your instinct is to blow up.

_____

_____

2. Sometimes we regress to some of our automatic parenting techniques, even when we've been using 1-2-3 Magic for quite a while. How do you recover after you've slipped up in front of your kids? What do you do if you find yourself screaming at one of them instead of calmly counting?

_____

_____

CHAPTER SUMMARY

1. The effectiveness of the counting method comes from your ability to administer it correctly.
2. Remember to explain to your children—when necessary—and then keep quiet. If you have to count, remember to do it calmly, with no emotion in your voice. You'll be amazed how effective it is when your kids begin to listen to you!

12

ESTABLISHING POSITIVE ROUTINES

How to Motivate Your Children to Do the Things They Need to Do

Chapter Overview

After getting a handle on Stop behavior, now it is time to tackle Start behavior. Start behaviors are those actions you want your children to *start* doing, like cleaning their rooms and completing homework. In this chapter, you will learn how to train your children by helping them master routines. You will find out how to define and rehearse procedures to establish routines, and you will discover seven Start behavior tactics to use in your training.

Questions about Chapter 12

1. What are the first two steps to establishing routines?
2. What are three problems that can occur with requests?
3. What is the basic concept of the docking system?
4. What are a few situations where natural consequences might be appropriate?
5. When should you use artificial reinforcers?

Case Study

Brenda has been struggling with her strong-willed son Josiah. He's tough to wake up in the morning, and getting him to go to bed at night is even more difficult. Josiah is in the third grade, and now Brenda has to get him to do his homework. She has tried counting Josiah. The counting does have some impact, but the effect doesn't last long. Brenda often resorts to yelling, but she then feels very guilty afterward.

WHAT WOULD YOU SUGGEST?

1. What would you tell Brenda about her use of counting in these situations?

_____

_____

_____

2. What are some tactics that might help Josiah get into a good morning and bedtime routine?

_____

_____

_____

Quick Tip

With Start behavior, you can use more than one tactic at a time for a particular problem. You may even come up with some of your own strategies. Remember: Train the kids to do what you want, or keep quiet!

How Are Things at Your House?

On scale of 1 to 5 (with 1 being TERRIBLE and 5 being PERFECT), how are you doing with motivating your children in the Start behavior category?

TERRIBLE ·· PERFECT

| 1 | 2 | 3 | 4 | 5 |

What is your biggest Start behavior problem? How are you trying to manage it?

_____

_____

Putting 1-2-3 Magic into Action with Your Family

Once you've mastered the 1-2-3 counting procedure, it's time to turn your attention to training your kids in Start behavior. Turn back to chapter 2 (page 9) and look at your list of Start behaviors. What are some tactics that might be useful for each of the areas you listed?

START BEHAVIOR	POSSIBLE TACTIC
_____	_____
_____	_____
_____	_____
_____	_____

Troubleshooting Exercise

Anytime you are training your kids for a Start behavior, you can expect some testing and manipulation as they resist doing chores and other activities they may not want to do. What kinds of testing do you expect, and how will you handle it when your kids try to get you off track?

_____

_____

CHAPTER SUMMARY

1. Start behavior requires more motivation from children than Stop behavior.
2. Use counting to manage Stop behavior for a week to ten days before tackling Start behavior.
3. Be creative with encouraging Start behavior.
4. Train the kids to do what you want, or keep quiet!

Your Seven Start Behavior Tactics

1. Praise (Positive Reinforcement)
2. Simple Requests
3. Kitchen Timers
4. The Docking System
5. Natural Consequences
6. Charting
7. Counting Variation

Keep your thinking cap on—and good luck!

13

GETTING UP AND OUT
IN THE MORNING

Building the Routines That Start Your Day

Chapter Overview

Getting kids up in the morning can be quite a chore. Many people—both parents and kids—are naturally crabby when they wake up. Combine this crabbiness with the extra pressure of having to be somewhere on time, and you have a recipe for disaster. In this chapter, you will learn how to use several tactics to train your children to get up and out in the morning. Hang in there! Your mornings could roll along more smoothly in just a few days.

Questions about Chapter 13

1. What does this chapter suggest you do before you design your morning routine?
2. What can you expect from younger children in the mornings?
3. What tactics can you use to help train four- and five-year-olds to get up in the mornings?
4. When can you use counting in the mornings?
5. How do you train older kids to take responsibility for getting up?

Case Study

Rena is having a tough time getting her two kids, ages ten and five, up and out in the morning. Currently she is using the wake-'em-up-and-fuss-at-them-until-they-are-ready plan. Rena desperately would like more peace and more cooperation in the mornings. The more she gets upset with her children, the worse they seem to do. She's tried counting, and it doesn't seem to do the job. The stress of the daily morning chaos makes it hard for Rena to concentrate when she gets to work. Her recent performance review was merely satisfactory.

WHAT WOULD YOU SUGGEST?

1. What would you tell Rena about her use of counting in this situation?

_____

_____

_____

2. What tactics could you use to train the younger child? What tactics would be most appropriate for the older child?

_____

_____

_____

Quick Tip

Tell your older kids that from now on, getting up and out in the morning is going to be their responsibility—totally. You will neither supervise nor nag them. At first, your children will not believe you are serious, but they *will* believe you are serious after you've let them get burned a few times. What's your chief job in all this? It's keeping quiet.

How Are Things at Your House?

What plan are you currently using to get your kids up and out in the mornings?

_____

_____

On scale of 1 to 5 (with 1 being TERRIBLE and 5 being PERFECT), how would you rate your attempts at getting your kids up and out in the morning?

TERRIBLE				PERFECT
1	2	3	4	5

Putting 1-2-3 Magic into Action with Your Family

1. If getting your kids going in the morning is a challenge, outline a plan of action based on this chapter to train your kids for a better morning routine.

_____

_____

_____

2. Do you have a good morning routine for getting yourself going? What is it?

_____

_____

_____

Troubleshooting Exercise

Natural consequences can be very effective but difficult to implement. If you are considering using this technique, take a few minutes to think through the different scenarios that may come up. Also, think about the manipulation you might encounter from your kids. List the ways you plan to handle the kids' testing tactics.

_____

_____

_____

_____

_____

CHAPTER SUMMARY

1. Preschoolers will need lots of help and praise to establish positive morning routines.
2. Young children respond well to praise, charting, and timers.
3. Older children benefit from natural consequences, but don't expect the experience to be fun!

14
CLEANING UP AND CHORES
Tips for Getting Your Kids to Clean Up after Themselves

Chapter Overview

Kids' messiness drives many parents crazy. Their children's rooms are in disarray, their shoes and toys are all over the house, and the kids never seem to do their simple chores. Parents need to remember that jobs like cleaning rooms and picking up do not come naturally to kids. Children must be trained to accomplish these tasks. In this chapter, you will learn some great principles to help get rooms cleaned, the house picked up, and chores completed. And best of all, no nagging, yelling, or parental outbursts are required!

Questions about Chapter 14

1. Does counting work to get kids to clean up their rooms?
2. Which room-cleaning option do you like most? Why?
3. What tactics are suggested for getting things picked up?
4. What strategy can be used to encourage younger children to complete their chores?
5. What is the best advice in regard to owning and caring for a pet?

Case Study

Allison is fed up with the state of her house. She has three children who are five, nine, and eleven. The kids' rooms are a wreck, toys are all over the house, and the dog would starve if Allison relied on the kids' promises to feed him. She is tired of reminding, nagging, and fussing. She and her husband have talked and decided things need to change. The problem is that Allison is not sure what to do.

WHAT DO YOU SUGGEST?

1. How would you counsel Allison in this situation?

    _____

    _____

2. What tactics would you begin with to get the children into a routine of cleaning their rooms and completing their chores?

    _____

    _____

Key Concept

Your kids do not have a right to mess up your entire house! Tell the children that by a certain time every day, anything of theirs that you find lying around will be confiscated and unavailable to them until a certain time the following day. Pick up the kids' things without grumbling or lecturing. You'll soon find that before the magic hour comes each day, they will be scurrying around to salvage their possessions.

How Are Things at Your House?

On scale of 1 to 5 (with 1 being TERRIBLE and 5 being PERFECT), how would you rate your attempts at getting your children to clean their rooms and complete their chores?

TERRIBLE ·································· PERFECT

| 1 | 2 | 3 | 4 | 5 |

Which chore or task do you want to focus on getting your kids to do first?

_____

_____

_____

Putting 1-2-3 Magic into Action with Your Family

1. In the area that you want to begin with, what tactics will you use to train your children?

_____

_____

_____

2. How and when will you begin this process?

_____

_____

_____

Troubleshooting Exercise

Some parents have very high expectations when it comes to keeping things neat and organized. Remember that cleaning, chores, and picking up are learned behaviors. So give yourself and your kids a break. Develop a plan, allow some time for your kids to get into the routine, and be sure to praise their accomplishments.

_____

_____

_____

CHAPTER SUMMARY

1. Children must be trained to clean up their rooms, pick up after themselves, and do chores.
2. Close the door, the weekly cleanup, and daily charting are good strategies for cleaning rooms.
3. The kitchen timer, the docking system, and the garbage bag method work well for picking up.
4. Praise, family meetings, charting, and the docking system are good strategies for everyday chores.

15

SURVIVING SUPPERTIME

What to Do When Your Kids Won't Eat

Chapter Overview

Dinnertime is supposed to be good family time. It's a chance for family members to talk about their day and just enjoy being together. However, with picky eaters, sibling rivalry, and tired parents, this meal can turn into a culinary catastrophe. In this chapter, you will learn how to encourage your picky eaters and bring a more relaxed atmosphere to your mealtimes. With just a little planning, eating supper can be a pleasant experience. Indigestion is not fun, but good food should be!

Questions about Chapter 15

1. When is it appropriate to count at the dinner table?
2. What is the basic of idea of using a kitchen timer to get kids into an eating routine?
3. If you use a kitchen timer, what happens to the food when the timer rings?
4. What is the Three-out-of-Four Rule?
5. How can you use the Divide-and-Conquer Routine to occasionally improve your family's experience of mealtimes?

Case Study

Bill dreads coming home for dinner. Bill and Brenda's younger son, Joey, has become a handful at the table. Brenda spends most of the mealtime fussing at Joey and trying to get him to eat. Bill then fusses at Brenda for fussing at Joey. Bill and Brenda's older son eats quickly and leaves to avoid the conflict. This routine can go on for as long as an hour. The parents have tried letting Joey not eat supper, but then bedtime becomes whining time since he's still hungry.

WHAT WOULD YOU SUGGEST?

1. Based on this chapter, what could Bill and Brenda do to better manage their picky eater?

_____

_____

2. What ideas could they try that would make mealtimes better for their older son?

_____

_____

Quick Tip

Try this with your finicky eaters. Give the kids super-small portions and then set the timer for twenty minutes. If the children finish before the timer goes off, they get their dessert. You may not nag or prompt—the timer will do that for you.

Key Concept

Who says you have to eat dinner together every single night of the year? Consider having some special nights where each person eats wherever she wishes. Or—better yet—have some nights where one parent takes one child out to eat. It's different, and it's fun!

How Are Things at Your House?

On scale of 1 to 5 (1 being TERRIBLE and 5 being PERFECT), how would you rate your mealtimes?

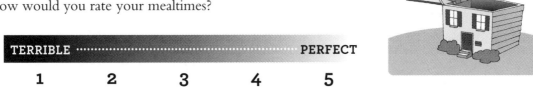

TERRIBLE	··	PERFECT

1   2   3   4   5

If your mealtimes are not rated as a 5, which tactics do you think would work best for your family?

_____

_____

Putting 1-2-3 Magic into Action with Your Family

1. If you have more than one child and your mealtimes have been chaotic, would you consider the Divide-and-Conquer idea occasionally? If so, when and how will you implement this strategy?

   _____

   _____

2. How would *your* kids feel about the Divide-and-Conquer notion?

   _____

   _____

Troubleshooting Exercise

Many parents forget the No Talking and No Emotion Rules at mealtimes. Whichever tactic you choose, remember not to nag or prompt. Allow the strategies to do the work. And remember, relax. No child we know of has died of starvation when good food was available.

How was suppertime managed by your parents? Can any of their ideas help you?

_____

_____

_____

CHAPTER SUMMARY

For picky eaters, try:

1. Small portions and a kitchen timer
2. The Three-out-of-Four Rule

For more peace at mealtimes, occasionally try:

1. The Divide-and-Conquer Routine
2. Not talking

16

TACKLING THE HOMEWORK PROBLEM

What to Do When Schoolwork Is Taking Over Your Family

Chapter Overview

Homework civil wars can make school nights miserable for the whole family. Everyone starts dreading after-school and evening times. Though there are no easy answers, there are ways to make homework time more tolerable and productive. In this chapter, you will learn about some of these methods, including why routine is critical and how natural consequences can sometimes do the trick. You will also discover several other strategies that can help make schoolwork times more bearable for you and your children. Homework is a permanent and necessary evil. Start getting control of it today!

Questions about Chapter 16

1. How can routine cut down on homework issues?
2. How can natural consequences help with schoolwork struggles?
3. What is the main rule with the Positive-Negative-Positive (PNP) Method?
4. What is the Magic Point in charting for homework?
5. What is the Rough Checkout?

Case Study

Dan and Judy's son, Justin, has struggled with homework for years. Judy tries to help Justin each evening, but she usually comes away frustrated. Justin often forgets his homework assignments and often starts assignments late in the evening when he does have them. Dan is usually the heavy, but is tired of arguing with Justin. Lately, Dan and Judy have tried staying out of it, but Justin's grades have plummeted. The parents are frustrated and not sure what to do.

WHAT WOULD YOU SUGGEST?

1. What would be your first suggestion to Dan and Judy?

_____

_____

_____

2. Would charting be useful in this situation? Why or why not?

_____

_____

_____

Quick Tip

The first thing out of your mouth when your child shows you her homework must be something positive—even if it's just that she brought her work to you. And remember: 8:00 p.m. is no time to strive for academic perfection!

How Are Things at Your House?

On scale of 1 to 5 (1 being TERRIBLE and 5 being PERFECT), how would you rate your homework and practice routines?

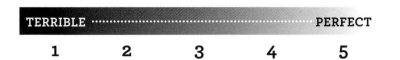

| TERRIBLE | ⋯⋯⋯⋯⋯⋯⋯⋯⋯⋯⋯⋯ | PERFECT |

1   2   3   4   5

What is the most difficult part of homework time in your house?

_____

_____

Putting 1-2-3 Magic into Action with Your Family

1. If your homework routine is not rated as a 5, which Start behavior tactics do you think would work best for your child?

_____

_____

_____

2. How will you implement these new tactics?

_____

_____

_____

Troubleshooting Exercise

If your child experiences chronic homework problems, you will need to take a closer look at why he or she is having such a hard time. You may need to set up a time with your child's teacher or counselor to discuss a possible learning disability or other impairment. Don't wait! The sooner you diagnose a problem, the sooner you can help your child succeed.

CHAPTER SUMMARY

1. Routine is critical.
2. Develop a strategy and stick with it.
3. Try to get homework done before dinner.
4. You can also use homework strategies for practicing musical instruments.

Homework Helpers

1. No spontaneous requests!
2. Natural consequences
3. The Positive-Negative-Positive (PNP) Method
4. The Rough Checkout
5. Charting

17

GOING TO BED—AND STAYING THERE!

How to Handle the Nightmare of Bedtime

Chapter Overview

Putting kids to bed and keeping them there can be a daily nightmare for many frazzled parents. Often a parent and child can get locked in a battle that ends with arguing and screaming. Then no one feels like sleeping! However, there is a better way. In this chapter, you will learn about the Basic Bedtime Method, which can actually make bedtime an enjoyable experience. You will also find some tips on how to handle kids getting out of bed and the inevitable nighttime waking that most kids go through.

Questions about Chapter 17

1. What is the first thing you must do in the Basic Bedtime Method?
2. If you are having trouble thinking of all the things that need to be done to get ready for bed, what does *1-2-3 Magic* suggest?
3. What are the purposes of the special time before bed?
4. How do you handle a child getting out of bed?
5. What are the basic steps to handle nighttime waking?

Case Study

Christy has a terrible time with her son, Ben, most evenings. Her struggle begins with homework and continues through trying to get him to go to bed. Lately, she has offered Ben the option of later bedtimes if he finishes his homework. The trouble is that no bedtime is late enough. He still wants to stay up later. Christy is very frustrated and doesn't know what to do.

WHAT WOULD YOU SUGGEST?

1. Do you think changing the bedtime is a good idea?

_____

_____

_____

2. What would you suggest to Christy for getting Ben to bed?

_____

_____

_____

Caution

Never forget one very important fact: If a child won't stay in bed at bedtime, the longer he is up, and the farther away he gets from his bedroom, the more reinforcement he will get from that activity. Your job? Cut him off at the pass.

How Are Things at Your House?

On a scale of 1 to 5, how would you rate your current bedtime ritual (1 means it is TERRIBLE, and 5 means that it is PERFECT)?

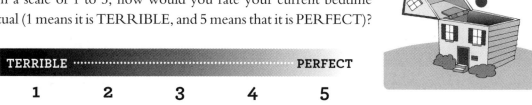

TERRIBLE	PERFECT
1 2 3 4 5	

Do you have any problems keeping your child in the bed after bedtime or during the night? Explain.

_____

_____

_____

Putting 1-2-3 Magic into Action with Your Family

1. What are some ideas you could implement to improve your family's bedtime plan?

_____

_____

2. If you have a spouse or partner, how would you use more free time together in the evening?

_____

_____

Troubleshooting Exercises

1. If you have more than one child, bedtime can be even more of a challenge. You may need to stagger bedtimes or alternate certain tasks with your spouse. Write your plans here.

_____

_____

_____

2. What are the bedtimes you will pick for each of your kids?

_____

_____

_____

CHAPTER SUMMARY

1. Set a bedtime and stick to it.
2. Use the Basic Bedtime Method to get kids to bed.
3. The longer a child stays up, the more reinforcement he gets and the more difficult it will be to get him back to bed.
4. No lights or talking during nighttime waking.

18

MANAGING YOUR EXPECTATIONS

What You Can Expect from Your Child, and When

Chapter Overview

Lots and lots of parent-child conflict is caused not so much by kids' misbehaving as by parents' not knowing exactly **when** they should expect **what** from their children. In other words, we parents can get impatient, sometimes expecting too much too soon (sitting still, listening) or other times seeing normal behavior (sibling rivalry, tantrums) as pathological. Parents may see their children as uncooperative, stubborn, or oppositional, when in reality the kids are just acting their age.

Questions about Chapter 18

1. "Two-year-olds don't read novels!" Explain the significance of this statement.
2. What percentage of two- to three-year-olds have daily tantrums?
3. At what age do most kids stop taking naps?
4. How often do three- to seven-year-olds fight?

Case Study

Marc takes his two-year-old son, Clark, to the grocery store. In the checkout line, Clark asks for some chocolate, and Marc says no. Clark throws a huge fit, yelling and thrashing around like a wild man in the grocery cart. Marc reprimands his son, then explains again why the boy can't have candy (it's too close to lunch), then yells himself. Marc is totally embarrassed. When he gets home, Marc asks his wife, Clare, to call the pediatrician to find out if they need to see a psychologist.

WHAT WOULD YOU SUGGEST?

1. What is Clark's problem?

_____

_____

_____

2. What is Marc's problem?

_____

_____

_____

3. What is Clare's problem?

_____

_____

_____

How Are Things at Your House?

1. Which of the Dirty Dozen issues has been the biggest problem at your house? How have you managed it in the past? How will 1-2-3 Magic help you to manage this problem differently in the future?

_____

_____

_____

2. If you have a spouse or partner living with you, do you frequently have differences of opinion regarding how to react to and manage the Dirty Dozen issues?

_____

_____

_____

Putting 1-2-3 Magic into Action with Your Family

Pick a Start behavior problem from the twelve items listed in chapter 18. Now look at the Start behavior tactics in chapter 2, and make a plan for how to manage that behavior. How will realizing that this behavior is normal affect your actions or feelings?

_____

_____

Pick a Stop behavior problem from the twelve items listed in chapter 18. Now look at the Stop behavior strategy (counting) in chapter 5, and make a plan for how to manage that behavior. How will realizing that this behavior is normal affect your actions or feelings?

_____

_____

Troubleshooting Exercise

Have you ever been frustrated by your kids' inability to listen to even simple commands or instructions? Describe how you might change your *attitude* toward this problem, and specifically, how you will manage it from now on in different situations.

_____

_____

_____

_____

CHAPTER SUMMARY

1. Identify three problem areas where your expectations for your children might be a part of the problem.
2. Avoid feeling like your kids are "out to get you" when they misbehave, and also don't feel their misbehavior is your fault.
3. Use well-thought-out routines to gently train kids.
4. Lecturing, nagging, and arguing are not well-thought-out routines!

PART V

Strengthening Your Relationships with Your Children

Parenting Job 3

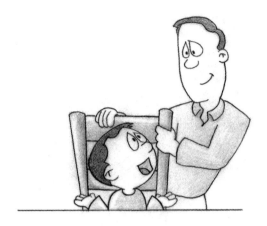

19

SYMPATHETIC LISTENING

Why It's Important to Hear What Your Children Have to Say

Chapter Overview

Your children will sometimes surprise you with their comments. Your daughter, for example, screams, "I hate school! The work is too hard!" Your immediate reaction may be to scream right back, "Hey! Don't yell at me! That's 1!" Think about this for a minute, though. Your daughter is clearly frustrated and angry. Is she screaming at you, or is she screaming to you? There is a definite difference. While screaming may not be the best way to deal with her frustration, keep in mind that she's a kid! Most kids don't know how to effectively express their negative emotions. Right now, your daughter needs a sympathetic listener, not a disciplinarian.

Questions about Chapter 19

1. List the three steps of sympathetic listening.
2. What two things does sympathetic listening try to accomplish?

3. How should you decide when to listen and when to count?

4. Why is sympathetic listening good for children's self-esteem?

Case Study

Dan's daughter, Tina, has been outside playing with friends. Dan has just gotten home from work and is finally beginning to relax a bit when he starts to hear voices raised outside. Suddenly Tina runs in the front door and slams it shut. She screams, "I HATE Jenny! She's always trying to take my friends away from me!" Tina knows not to slam the door, and Dan definitely doesn't appreciate her screaming at him. He's tired from work, which makes his annoyance even more pronounced. He looks at her sternly and says, "That's 1."

WHAT WOULD YOU DO?

1. In the same situation, what would you have said to Tina instead of "That's 1"?

_____

_____

2. How likely is it that Tina will continue to come to her father with her problems in the future?

_____

_____

Caution

You are a **good listener** if, while your child is talking, you are sincerely trying to understand what he is saying. You are a **bad listener** if, while your child is talking, you are preparing your rebuttal.

How Are Things at Your House?

1. Do you think you are generally a sympathetic listener?

_____

_____

2. Can you think of a circumstance when you have responded to one of your children the way Dan did to Tina? If so, describe the situation.

_____

_____

Putting 1-2-3 Magic into Action with Your Family

1. Do you tend to worry unnecessarily? Does your spouse/parenting partner tend to do this as well?

_____

_____

_____

2. List three things that you can tell yourself when you begin to worry too much that can help you to backpedal, see the bigger picture, and avoid over-parenting.

_____

_____

_____

Troubleshooting Exercises

Keep in mind that the older your kids get, the more you are going to want them to come to you with their problems. Their problems only become bigger and much more serious as they enter their teen years. You want your children to know from a young age that you are a safe person for them to come to when they are troubled.

If you become a good sympathetic listener, you will be pleasantly surprised to learn that your kids will enjoy talking to you, allowing you to better strengthen your relationships with them.

CHAPTER SUMMARY

1. We **listen** to problems, and we **count** attacks. It's important to recognize the difference.
2. You don't want your children to feel that they will get yelled at every time they try to discuss unpleasant situations or feelings, even if they aren't handling their emotions exactly as you would like them to.

Over-parenting is the opposite of listening!

20

THE DANGERS OF OVER-PARENTING

Knowing When to Let Your Kids Think for Themselves

Chapter Overview

Sometimes referred to as "helicopter parenting," over-parenting is a good way to do some serious damage to a relationship with a child. Over-parenting usually consists of unnecessary disciplinary, cautionary, or otherwise corrective comments that come more from a parent's own anxiety than anything else. Since kids have a ferocious desire to become independent, unnecessary and anxious comments from a parent usually make the children irritated.

Questions about Chapter 20

1. How would you explain the Anxious Parent, Angry Child syndrome?
2. List two reasons why over-parenting comments are often unnecessary.
3. Why is independence so important to children?
4. Does the following statement make sense? Parents want two things from their children—compliance and independence.

Case Study

Nine-year-old Michelle is excitedly heading off to friend's birthday party at 3:00 p.m. Her mother stops her in the doorway and reminds her not to be too loud, not to eat too much cake, to be sure and share, to be sure and thank her friend's mother before she leaves, and to not forget her coat when she returns home.

WHAT WOULD YOU DO?

1. What advice would you have for Michelle's mother?

_____

_____

2. How do you think Michelle felt after receiving her mother's reminders?

_____

_____

How Are Things at Your House?

1. Do you ever feel you talk too much to your children when you are very anxious or nervous?

_____

_____

2. When you were growing up, did you ever feel your mom and dad over-parented you?

_____

_____

Putting 1-2-3 Magic into Action with Your Family

Using what you learned in chapter 20, describe what you will do differently in your own home to avoid the Anxious Parent, Angry Child syndrome. If you have a spouse or partner, consider the possibility of giving each other some gentle and positive feedback regarding times when you both feel that anxious and unnecessary comments are being made to the children.

_____

_____

Troubleshooting Exercise

Another way of looking at over-parenting is by examining how often you give your kids *chronic, unwarranted supervision*. The opposite of chronic, unwarranted supervision is known as *weaning*. For example, is your intervention still necessary for issues such as homework, bedtime, brushing teeth, and chores? How can you help your kids become independent—like, totally!—in these areas?

_____

_____

CHAPTER SUMMARY

1. Over-parenting involves unnecessary, anxious comments directed at kids.
2. Over-parenting usually makes kids irritated.
3. The opposite of over-parenting is weaning.
4. Your long-term goal is your children's independence from you!

21

REAL MAGIC: ONE-ON-ONE FUN

The Best Thing You Can Do for Your Kids

Chapter Overview

Having fun with another human being is at the center of all relationships. In fact, any relationship that we *choose* to enter into (friendship, romance, and so on) usually begins because we find that we have fun with that other person! Having fun with your child—just the two of you—can be magical. It's one of the most important things you can do for your relationship. When you seek your child out to say, "Hey, let's play a game!" what your child hears is, "Hey, I like you and I think you're really cool to hang out with!" He feels valued and special. There is no greater gift that you can give to your child.

Questions about Chapter 21

1. Why is having fun with your child important for a positive relationship with her?
2. What are two reasons why family fun can be difficult?
3. Why is it important to find time for one-on-one fun, as opposed to always having family fun?

4. Why is it important to find an activity that *both you and your child* enjoy doing?

5. What are some examples of ways to have simple, inexpensive one-on-one fun?

Case Study

Susan's eight-year-old son, Trevor, walks into the kitchen complaining that he's bored. It's almost the end of summer, and most of the free-time activities that he usually engages in are getting stale and boring—except for one! Trevor loves to play with his Star Wars action figures anywhere, anytime. Susan suggests to Trevor that he go play with those, but he responds that it's no fun alone and none of his friends are home. "Will you play with me, Mom?"

If there is one thing that Susan detests, it's playing with Star Wars action figures. She has no idea how to pretend the way she's supposed to, and it always ends up with Trevor getting frustrated with her for "not doing it right." On the other hand, she hasn't spent any one-on-one fun time with him lately, and she supposes that this could fill the bill. She goes to play with him, but as predicted, she does it "wrong," and he ends up getting annoyed with her. She's happy to be finished with it—she hates that game anyway!

WHAT WOULD YOU DO?

1. Does the activity above count as one-on-one shared fun?

_____

2. What should Susan do about the problem?

_____

_____

_____

_____

Quick Tip

To like your kids, you must enjoy them regularly. And for them to respond well to your discipline, they must enjoy and like you too. That means only one thing: You'd better find regular time to play with your youngsters!

How Are Things at Your House?

Think of your children one at a time. On a scale of 1 to 5 (1 being NOT OFTEN AT ALL and 5 being VERY OFTEN), assign a number to each child according to how often the two of you have one-on-one fun on a regular basis.

NOT OFTEN AT ALL ·· VERY OFTEN

| 1 | 2 | 3 | 4 | 5 |

If it seems one of your children is getting "less" of you, or conversely, that one of your children is getting "more" of you, think about why that may be. What can you do to even things up?

_____

_____

_____

Putting 1-2-3 Magic into Action with Your Family

1. Write lists of five things (one list for each of your children) that you could do to have fun together. Remember that what is fun for one of your children may not be fun for another!

CHILD	CHILD	CHILD
_____	_____	_____
_____	_____	_____
_____	_____	_____
_____	_____	_____
_____	_____	_____

2. When you look at your family's lifestyle and schedule, how often do you think you can manage to spend thirty minutes of uninterrupted fun time with each of your children? Daily? Weekly? Monthly? Is this often enough? Do you need to reprioritize a bit?

_____

_____

Troubleshooting Exercises

1. Sometimes your relationship with your child is a bit rocky. It can be difficult to have shared fun with someone you argue with anytime either of you opens your mouth! However, this is the child who probably needs the time with you most of all. Name an activity that can be fun but that really requires minimal interaction (or opportunity for conflict).

_____

_____

2. Sometimes, money can be an issue. Remember that shared fun can be as simple and inexpensive as catching fireflies together. One-on-one fun doesn't have to cost you a dime! List some fun and inexpensive activities.

_____

_____

_____

_____

CHAPTER SUMMARY

Any two people who make the time to regularly have fun together will have a healthy rapport. It's one of the most important things that you can do for your relationship with your child!

22

SOLVING PROBLEMS TOGETHER

Why It's Better to Work as a Team

Chapter Overview

Wouldn't it be nice if we could all live peacefully together all of the time? Too bad life doesn't work that way! With busy schedules, financial pressures, sibling rivalry, and a whole host of other dynamics, peace is sometimes hard to maintain in a family. One way to facilitate peace and foster much more independence in your children is to have regular family meetings. These sometimes not-so-much-fun meetings can solve many of a family's daily problems. In this chapter, you will learn how to run a family meeting and how to conduct a one-on-one conversation with your child.

Questions about Chapter 22

1. What does it mean to move from a benevolent dictatorship to an "almost but not quite" democracy?
2. Why should you have family meetings?

3. What are the basic steps to a family meeting?
4. Why is it important not to talk to a child during a disciplinary episode?
5. Do you ever have a one-on-one meeting with a child to try to solve a problem?

Case Study

Casey tried a family meeting, but it did not go well. Her three-year-old child kept interrupting, and her nine-year-old twin girls just argued with each other. Casey wanted to involve her children in some family decisions, but they just didn't seem to be interested. Casey finally counted the girls and sent them to their rooms. She really would like to use family meetings, but she thinks they won't work for her family.

WHAT WOULD YOU SUGGEST?

1. What problems do you see in the case study that might have contributed to the failed meeting?

_____

_____

2. What guidelines could Casey implement that might help a family meeting work for her?

_____

_____

_____

_____

Quick Tip

Many parents agree that a family meeting is one of the most *aggravating* and one of the most *effective* things you can do with your children. Don't ever expect anyone to want to come!

How Are Things at Your House?

1. What are some specific issues that your family could address in a family meeting?

_____

_____

_____

2. How often do you discuss serious issues with your children individually?

_____

_____

Putting 1-2-3 Magic into Action with Your Family

1. When would be a good time for you to call a family meeting?

   Day: _____ Time: _____

2. What issues might be appropriate for one-on-one meetings for each of your children?

_____

_____

_____

_____

_____

_____

Troubleshooting Exercises

Family meetings can easily break down if you are not careful. One thing to watch out for is one child becoming the scapegoat. Be careful to keep the meeting focused on the issues and not on a particular person.

Pay attention to your own tolerance for family meetings. Can you go over an hour and remain patient and calm?

In a one-on-one meeting with a child, it's important for you to be a good listener first. Bite your tongue until you completely understand what they are trying to say.

CHAPTER SUMMARY

1. Keep family meetings short and focused. You'll find they are a useful tool in teaching your children valuable life skills!
2. Use a one-on-one meeting when you want to discuss an issue privately with one of your youngsters.
3. Family meetings and one-on-one meetings are not always fun. But they help prepare your kids for one of life's ultimate challenges...**living with someone else!**

PART VI

Enjoying Your New Family Life

23

STAYING CONSISTENT

You Will Make Some Mistakes—and That's Okay!

Chapter Overview

Sometimes when things go well in our lives, we forget the times when they weren't going so great. This is especially true of parenting. You're probably going through this workbook now because you are having some rough times. After you have begun tackling your three parenting jobs, though, things are likely to get better pretty quickly. This is great news! But what happens after your life gets a bit easier? You may slip—or "fall off the wagon"—and forget to use some of the strategies you learned in *1-2-3 Magic*. There are several reasons this may happen, but there are also some easy ways to get right back on track.

Questions about Chapter 23

1. In *1-2-3 Magic*, what does the term "slipping" mean?
2. List three reasons that slipping can occur over the long term.
3. List three emotional obstacles that may cause slipping.
4. How does one recover from short-term slipping?
5. How does one recover from long-term slipping?

Case Study

Mike and his wife, Anne, have been successfully using 1-2-3 Magic for many months. Their lives had gotten so much easier for a while. In the past weeks, though, Mike has noticed that chaos is beginning to take hold again, and it's annoying him. Mike and Anne are not counting their children as much, but they are talking and yelling more.

One Sunday afternoon, Mike is lying on the couch watching football. It's the only relaxation he gets all week, and he needs it! He hears a fight brewing in one of the kids' rooms. He is furious. All he asks for is a few hours of peace, one day a week! He heads upstairs, screaming the whole way. He'll take care of these kids!

WHAT WOULD YOU SUGGEST?

1. What is the real problem that this family is facing?

_____

_____

2. How should Mike handle this situation?

_____

_____

_____

_____

Quick Tip
When you're doing nine things at once, who can remember the No Talking and No Emotion Rules? **You can!**

How Are Things at Your House?

1. Which of the emotional obstacles currently give you the most trouble when you're dealing with your children?

_____

_____

2. Write about a specific instance when this particular emotional obstacle has been a problem for you.

_____

_____

_____

Putting 1-2-3 Magic into Action with Your Family

1. Are there any triggers for slipping coming up in your immediate future (such as a new baby, a vacation, or visitors)?

_____

2. If so, how will you prepare for this event?

_____

_____

_____

Troubleshooting Exercises

Falling off the wagon does not mean 1-2-3 Magic is not working. It simply means you're not working temporarily. Nobody's perfect!

As with anything that you take on in your life, preparation is key in parenting. Think ahead a few months or years. When you slip up in the future, write down how you will catch yourself and how you will handle the setback.

CHAPTER SUMMARY

1. A certain amount of slipping is normal. You are human! All you have to do when it happens is get back to basics.
2. If necessary, redo the Kickoff Conversation.
3. Enjoy the recovery!

24

YOUR HEALTHY, HAPPY FAMILY

How 1-2-3 Magic Will Change Your Life

Chapter Overview

You made it to the end! You now understand how to do your three parenting jobs. You're ready to control obnoxious behavior, encourage positive behavior, and build strong relationships with each of your children. Your life is about to change! No, your children will not sprout angel wings, but if you use 1-2-3 Magic correctly, you will find that a lot more peace (and fun!) is going to make its way into all of your lives.

Questions about Chapter 24

1. How will 1-2-3 Magic help to improve your children's self-esteem?
2. How will 1-2-3 Magic help to improve your self-esteem?
3. Why is parenting so exhausting for so many people?
4. List the ways in which 1-2-3 Magic will help you spend more positive time with your kids.
5. Are there any factors in your life that might sabotage your success?

Case Study

Carol's eight-year-old son, Tim, often struggles with his homework. He never wants to get started. Carol's next-door neighbor, Susan, can't stand the constant whining of her four-year-old daughter, Meghan. She seems to whine whenever she wants anything! Susan's brother, Mark, just told her over the phone that he is getting the feeling that he and his eleven-year-old son, Matthew, don't seem to enjoy each other's company so much anymore. This is starting to worry him a lot as the boy heads to adolescence.

WHAT WOULD YOU SUGGEST?

1. What should Carol do?

_____

2. What should Susan do?

_____

3. What should Mark do?

_____

4. Which parenting job is each of these parents dealing with?

_____

_____

_____

How Are Things at Your House?

1. Which of your children do you think will be the biggest challenge for you in implementing 1-2-3 Magic?

_____

Why? _____

_____

2. How will you work to manage your own feelings of frustration while helping this child
get with the program?

_____

_____

Putting 1-2-3 Magic into Action with Your Family

1. Why do you think that the first parenting step deals with handling Stop behaviors?

_____

_____

2. Which parenting step do you think will be the easiest for you to implement? Which one
will be the most challenging?

_____

_____

Troubleshooting Exercises

Remember that some slipping is normal! Keep in mind that certain family situations and just plain time passing can cause this to happen. What are some slipping triggers that you need to watch out for?

_____

_____

Although slipping may mean you're going through a difficult time, it does not mean there's something wrong with you or your family.

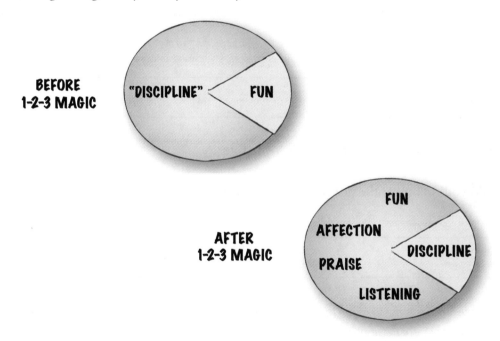

CHAPTER SUMMARY

Explain each diagram.

Now that you're ready to take back control of your home, everyone's lives will become calmer, happier, and easier.

Enjoy Your Kids!

1-2-3 Magic in Action

ILLUSTRATED STORIES AND QUESTIONS

Counting Obnoxious Behavior:
The Case of the Temper Tantrum Terrorist

Sibling Rivalry: *The Incredible Case of
the Traveling Troublemakers*

Encouraging Positive Routines:
The Case of Bedlam at Bedtime

Sympathetic Listening:
The Case of the Fickle Friends

COUNTING OBNOXIOUS BEHAVIOR

 When they start the 1-2-3 Magic program, many parents begin by simply counting obnoxious behavior for a few days to a week before they do anything with Parenting Jobs 2 and 3—encouraging good behavior and strengthening relationships. That's the way my husband and I handled it, and it was a good move!

In The Case of the Temper Tantrum Terrorist, you'll meet our five-year-old son, Zach. Before 1-2-3 Magic, this kid was a handful. While I've heard that many children (about 50 percent) will shape up in just a few days with counting, it took us about a week to make Zach a believer.

Here's our story. In the Before section, you'll see two bewildered parents. Then you'll sit in on our Thinking It Through process before we get around to handling our son After.

THE CASE OF THE TEMPER TANTRUM TERRORIST

APPLE PIE!!

I must admit, I don't like to think about our life before *1-2-3 Magic*. Our home was run by a five-year-old. If our Zach didn't get his way, he resorted to kicking, screaming, or crying. We spent so much time making sure Zach was happy that we remained miserable. Going to the store required both parents. Eating out was an exercise in futility, and neighborhood barbeques were politely declined.

One night we took a chance and went to a local restaurant...

BEFORE

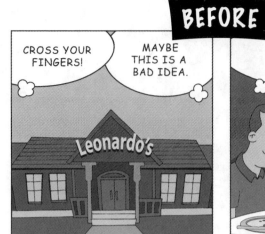

Maybe tonight would be our lucky night! The waitress returned.

Zach ordered chocolate cake.

As soon as the waitress left, though, he changed his mind.

BEFORE

Well, the first round went to Zach—in a sense. Actually, it didn't go to anybody, since we all wound up feeling miserable. You can't beat public humiliation for pure fun—and, believe me, we'd been through plenty of scenes like the one you just witnessed.

We just couldn't keep on going like this. We were getting discouraged, and we had to do something different. But exactly what was that "something" going to be? Usually the mom is the one to get the ball rolling with problems like this, and our house was no exception.

Feeling desperate, I decided to try a product that I thought at the time would be a long shot.

THINKING IT THROUGH

I had heard about *1-2-3 Magic*, and bought it the next day.

The book was describing our family.

THINKING IT THROUGH

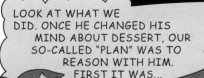

LOOK AT WHAT WE DID. ONCE HE CHANGED HIS MIND ABOUT DESSERT, OUR SO-CALLED "PLAN" WAS TO REASON WITH HIM. FIRST IT WAS...

ZACH, THE WAITRESS IS GONE. IT'S TOO LATE TO CHANGE YOUR MIND.

THEN WE TRIED THE BRILLIANT LINE...

DON'T YOU REMEMBER YOU LOVE CHOCOLATE CAKE!

FOLLOWED BY THE ALWAYS EFFECTIVE...

NOW DON'T ACT LIKE A BABY. IF YOU DON'T EAT YOUR CAKE, MOM AND DAD WILL!

AND FINALLY...

ZACH, SHSSH! THAT'S ENOUGH. PEOPLE ARE TRYING TO EAT!

SO WHAT'S WRONG WITH EXPLAINING? HE'S GOT TO UNDERSTAND...

NO! **WE'VE** GOT TO UNDERSTAND THAT OUR SON IS NOT 30 YEARS OLD. HE'S ONLY 5!!

WE WERE EXPECTING HIM—WHEN FACED WITH OUR DAZZLING LOGIC—TO IMMEDIATELY CALM DOWN AND SAY SOMETHING LIKE...

GEE, I NEVER LOOKED AT IT LIKE THAT BEFORE! THANKS FOR THE EXPLANATION.

After our talk, there were times when I thought my husband understood what I was saying, but most of the time I felt I wasn't getting anywhere. He hadn't read the book, so I got the *1-2-3 Magic* DVD (which I thought was just as good as the book). My husband hinted—but only hinted—that he might be willing to watch the DVD, but only if I wasn't in the room!

Why are adult males so hard to talk to? Zach's behavior remained awful. As far as I was concerned, we were still in a big pickle—stuck with nowhere to go.

Then one day a miracle occurred.

THINKING IT THROUGH

My husband actually watched the *1-2-3 Magic* DVD. And he liked it!

We practiced counting on each other.

THAT'S 2.

We whispered about our plans—Zach's suspicious eyes watched us.

I CAN BEAT THIS.

We had the Kickoff Conversation.

ZACH, WE'RE GOING TO DO SOME THINGS DIFFERENT AROUND HERE.

My husband and I were a team! We were ready for whatever he could throw at us.

AFTER

Ha! Little did we know! This is how the first night went.

WHAT'S FOR DINNER?

CHICKEN AND RICE.

EEEW! I HATE CHICKEN AND RICE!

ZACH, YOU ATE IT LAST WEEK.

I DID NOT! **I HATE IT!!** DO I HAVE TO EAT IT?

THAT'S 1.

MOM, DO I HAVE TOOOOO?

THAT'S 2.

COULD I HAVE SOMETHING ELSE?

THAT'S 3 TAKE 5.

Zach wouldn't go to his room, so I carried him. He threw a fit but amazingly stayed put.

NO!!!

AFTER

Once he calmed down, five minutes was counted. He came out with puffy eyes and ate his chicken and rice.

We were elated! The 1-2-3 worked! It would be easy sailing from here on out.

Not so fast. Right after dinner this scene took place.

AFTER

THAT'S 3, TAKE 5.

He was picked up and carried to his room. He screamed again.

BUT DAD!

Once in his room he lay on the floor. He was quiet! And then he took his bath!!

When my husband and I went to bed we were so excited. We did it!

But the next day was worse. And the day after was even worse than that.

WAAA! KABAM! NO!!

Zach spent 50% of his time in time-out.

AFTER

We heard it all...

Then one day about a week after we started, I gave him a "1" and he said...

Zach was finally a believer. For a long time he never hit 3.

My husband and I were feeling good. I suggested we try the restaurant again.

Things went well until Zach started whining about leaving. We counted—he shaped up.

We all left the restaurant in good spirits. It was a new life.

Since our "week from hell," things have been very different around our house. Our son now knows that when we say something, we mean business. No yelling, no empty threats. Sure, he still pushes the limits at times, but he doesn't get anywhere.

We've also advanced in our use of 1-2-3 Magic to the strategies for encouraging good behavior (like getting Zach to bed) and to doing things that reinforce the bond between us (like shared fun). Since we have learned how to control Zach's oppositional moments, it is so much easier to like him!

Keep in mind that when you start counting your kids, you may not have to go through a hell week like our family. But honestly, if the stories in this book had a tale of a youngster shaping up in just a few hours (which has happened many times!), you wouldn't believe it, would you?

We hope our harrowing tale has given you some encouragement!

Questions and Answers for You

Before they start the 1-2-3 Magic program, many parents are skeptical about whether this new method will work. Moms and dads can still be somewhat hesitant after reading the book or watching the DVDs.

There are several reasons why parents may feel doubtful before using 1-2-3 Magic. Let's look at four of these concerns, and then we'll ask you a few questions about what is known as the Little Adult Assumption.

CONCERN 1:
When frustrated, your child is ferocious!

Do you have a "Zach" at your house? What is he like when he doesn't get his way?

_____

_____

How does this affect your discipline?

_____

_____

_____

CONCERN 2:
You feel like you've already tried everything.

How many different discipline approaches have you tried? Which ones helped, and which were no help at all?*

_____

_____

_____

_____

*Guess what? Most parents who say "We've tried everything" have, in fact, done _nothing_ consistently.

CONCERN 3:
Counting seems too simple or too wimpy.

What was your first reaction to Mom's strategy in the scene above?

_____

_____

**What was Zach's first reaction? What was his
reaction to the second and third counts?**

_____

_____

_____

CONCERN 4:
We should be able to talk everything over with our kids.

Do you think Zach's father had a feeling of impending doom at this point?

_____

_____

**When your children are frustrated, how often do
your explanations resolve the problem?**

_____

_____

Other Questions...

What would you think if Zach had reacted like this to his parents' comments?

_____

_____

_____

Other Questions...

What is happening to Zach's *anger level* as the "conversation" continues?

_____

How will this affect the chances of his cooperating?

_____

Think about this...

WE HAD AN ODD SITUATION
WITH ZACH WHERE

MORE TALKING
produced
LESS COOPERATION

If talking sometimes makes matters worse in a
crisis, why do we parents continue to do it?

_____

_____

_____

And finally...

You may not be an expert in kids' testing and manipulation yet (chapter 10), but how many different testing tactics can you identify in the frame above?

_____

_____

_____

What are your children's favorite tactics for trying to get their way?

_____

_____

SIBLING RIVALRY

Parenting is a difficult and complicated job. Admit it now. It's a lot harder than you ever imagined it would be before you had kids! Once our little ones showed up in our house, there they were—period. No escape and no going out without a babysitter.

Before we had children, my husband and I imagined the warm, fuzzy, peaceful, and affectionate times we would have with our kids. But after several years of parenting experience, we quickly learned that we also had to manage whining, teasing, tantrums, messiness, and not wanting to go to bed.

We also found out that having two kids is a lot harder than one. Sibling rivalry is a chronic challenge, and it's one of the most aggravating things kids can do. Managing and minimizing kids' fighting is part of Parenting Job 1.

Check out this story...

One day, on our way home from the grocery store, my children were passing the time looking for pictures in the clouds. This is a favorites game of theirs, and I love hearing their creative ideas. On this particular day my six-year-old daughter suddenly said...

THE INCREDIBLE CASE OF THE TRAVELING TROUBLEMAKERS

Once we were off to the side of the road, I put my flashers on.

About a minute went by. I looked in my mirror and saw lights.

You guessed it. It was a police officer!

He came walking up to my door.

IS EVERYTHING OK, MA'AM?

I explained my children were fighting, so I pulled over and we were taking a time-out.

THAT'S A GOOD IDEA AND A SAFE ONE! HAVE A GOOD DAY.

He smiled, then just looked at the kids and waved to them. They seemed to be in shock!

It was silent the rest of the way home. They have not even attempted fighting in the car again—yet!

Questions for You

On a scale from 1 to 5, how aggravating
would this scene be for you?

NOT SO AGGRAVATING ·············· **VERY AGGRAVATING**

1   2   3   4   5

List three things this mother would like to say
(but should not say!) at this point:

_____

_____

_____

Questions for You

What two rules for managing sibling rivalry is Mom following here?

_____

_____

How is Mom feeling at this point? Why?

_____

_____

Questions for You

**Why did the policeman say
Mom's idea was a "safe one"?**

_____

_____

**How long do you think it will be until
these kids have another fight?**

_____

_____

ENCOURAGING POSITIVE ROUTINES

As you have learned from *1-2-3 Magic*, a big part of Parenting Job 2, encouraging good behavior, is establishing reasonable and consistent routines. Kids do much better when the tasks you want them to accomplish, like eating supper and homework, are carried out each day at the same time and pretty much in the same way.

One of the most critical daily routines is getting the kids to bed—and getting them to stay there. Mess this job up and everyone will pay dearly, not only in the evening but the next day as well. That's what happened to us. We had to learn the hard way how to do bedtime with our young daughter, but what a relief once we figured it out!

Here's our story...

We got angry, yelled and "laid down the law."

THAT'S ENOUGH YOUNG LADY! I DON'T WANT TO SEE YOU DOWNSTAIRS AGAIN!!

The following morning, both of us would be exhausted. We could barely get through the workday.

ZZ

We started arguing more and more with each other.

YOU PUT HER TO BED TONIGHT.

WHY ME? I WORKED JUST AS HARD AS YOU TODAY!

FINE! WONDERFUL!! APPARENTLY I HAVE TO DO EVERYTHING AROUND HERE!!!

Nothing seemed to satisfy our daughter except to stay in her room until she went to sleep.

Z

Obviously, we couldn't keep this nighttime routine up for very long. The funny thing was that we already had the *1-2-3 Magic* book, and we had been successfully using counting during the day with our daughter. But we didn't see how in the world counting would help us with our little girl's refusal to stay in bed.

Guess what? Counting is *not* supposed to be used for this problem. Counting is more for controlling obnoxious behavior. Going to bed and staying there is basically a positive behavior that has to be encouraged with other tactics. Where would we find those strategies?

We had to finish reading *1-2-3 Magic*! We had been so delighted with the results of counting that we hadn't gone any further. There was a separate chapter called "Going to Bed—and Staying There!" There we learned the Basic Bedtime Method. First we had to pick a bedtime and stick with it. Then, a half hour before bedtime, we would inform Lucy that it was time to get ready for bed. She had to do everything to get ready and then check in with one of us. However much time was left in the half hour was story time or just one-on-one talking time. Then it would be lights-out.

What about her getting up all the time? Some kids keep getting up because they don't want the fun of the day to end. Others get up because they're scared. The "cut them off at the pass" procedure would take care of either possibility.

When bedtime came, we kissed her goodnight and put on the night-light and floor fan.

One of us then sat in a chair in the doorway (with a good book) with our back to our daughter.

If she said something, we would not say anything back.

I THINK THERE'S A GORILLA IN THE CLOSET!

If she got up, we would do our "stern" look and guide her back to bed.

As many times as necessary!

The first few nights we couldn't read more than a couple of pages of our book.

After a few more nights, though, we were able to read a few pages.

We tried to stay quiet and calm!

OK. ONE MORE TIME.

Within two weeks, we could tuck her in and leave the room! Success!

Our energy returned during the day.

And we enjoyed each other again.

Questions for You

List two mistakes Dad is making right here.

1. _____

2. _____

What are the two main reasons kids don't like to go to bed or stay in bed?

_____

_____

Workbook

Questions for You

If you have a spouse or a partner, what effect does
child discipline have on your relationship?

_____

_____

_____

Why are the parents in this scene getting mad at each other?

_____

_____

Questions for You

What would Mom like to say in this scene?

_____

_____

What would happen if Mom did say something here?

_____

_____

_____

SYMPATHETIC LISTENING

A big piece of Parenting Job 3, strengthening your relationships with your children, is listening to what your kids have to say. You want to be a good listener when your children are happy and excited, but it's also important to be there for them when they're frustrated, sad, or upset.

Unfortunately, sympathetic listening is easier to describe than it is to do. Sometimes we don't have the time to listen. At other times, however, we simply don't remember to take the time when we really could.

In our next story, *The Case of the Fickle Friends*, you will see me mishandle a situation in which my son was temporarily upset with some of his neighborhood buddies. In the portion of the story called the *Wrong Way*, you'll see me being a lousy listener. In *Thinking It Through*, we'll take a look at what I messed up. Then we'll give you a chance to evaluate your own listening skills with your kids.

Finally, the *Right Way* section of our narrative will give me a chance to undo my mistake—an opportunity that doesn't always happen in real life!

THE CASE OF THE FICKLE FRIENDS

When my wife and I got our first house, we were thrilled to death. Not only did we have our own yard, but our kids would also have friends to play with. What wasn't so thrilling, however, was our introduction to the new and unfamiliar world of playtime politics.

THINKING IT THROUGH

As I watched my son walk away, I realized that I had just blown it. Although I was caught off guard, what I said and did simply made matters worse.

WELL DON'T BOTHER ME ABOUT IT. FIND SOMETHING ELSE TO DO.

He was looking for a little reassurance and support, but I was too busy and aggravated to provide it for him.

STOP WHINING. THAT'S 1.

GEE, THANKS DAD.

To make matters worse, I misused the strategy of counting. Not very sympathetic, was I!

HOW ARE THINGS AT YOUR HOUSE?

Kids can catch you off guard with some of their interruptions and outbursts. It's not always easy to be a good listener. As you just saw in our example, I did not do a good job of paying attention to my son when he was upset.

Think about your own life with your kids and rate yourself on our SYMPATHETIC LISTENING SCALE:

How often do you take time to listen?

RARELY   SOMETIMES   A LOT

How often do you ask sympathetic questions?

RARELY   SOMETIMES   A LOT

How often do you try to understand your kid's feelings?

RARELY   SOMETIMES   A LOT

Listening to your youngsters is important. It's important for children's self-esteem and it's important for you to know what your kids are thinking. Let's revisit **The Case of the Fickle Friends** and give me a second chance to do it right.

RIGHT WAY

Being angry is no crime.

A sympathetic question was a better way to start.

Here I turned around and took time to listen. I gave my son emotional support, but at the same time I let him solve his own problem.

Better ending. David's less upset, I'm less upset —most important—we're not mad at each other.

GOOD JOB, DAD!

WHAT WOULD YOU DO?

Now that you know a little more about active listening, here's a quiz. If you were the parent of the little girl in the frames below, what would you say in these two situations?

JENNY INVITED ME TO HER BIRTHDAY PARTY!

1

MY MUSIC TEACHER'S AN IDIOT!

2

1. _____

_____

_____

2. _____

_____

_____

APPENDIX

Further Reading and Resources

Emotional Intelligence

Borba, Michele. *Building Moral Intelligence: The Seven Essential Virtues That Teach Kids to Do the Right Thing*. San Francisco: Jossey-Bass, 2002.

Goleman, Daniel. *Emotional Intelligence: Why It Can Matter More Than IQ*. New York: Bantam Books, 2005.

Active Listening and Problem Solving

Faber, Adele, and Elaine Mazlish. *How to Talk So Kids Will Listen and Listen So Kids Will Talk*. New York: Scribner, 2012.

Ginott, Haim. *Between Parent and Child*. Revised and updated by Alice Ginott and H. Wallace Goddard. New York: Three Rivers Press, 2003.

Shure, Myra B. *I Can Problem Solve: An Interpersonal Cognitive Problem-Solving Program*. Champaign, IL: Research Press, 2001.

Childhood Emotional Problems

Chansky, Tamar E. *Freeing Your Child from Anxiety: Powerful, Practical Solutions to Overcome Your Child's Fears, Worries, and Phobias.* Updated edition. New York: Harmony Books, 2014.

Colorosco, Barbara. *The Bully, the Bullied, and the Bystander: From Preschool to High School—How Parents and Teachers Can Help Break the Cycle.* New York: William Morrow Paperbacks, 2009.

Turecki, Stanley, and Sarah Warnick. *The Emotional Problems of Normal Children: How Parents Can Understand and Help.* New York: Bantam Books, 1994.

Separation and Divorce

Philyaw, Deesha, and Michael D. Thomas. *Co-Parenting 101: Helping Your Kids Thrive in Two Households after Divorce.* Oakland, CA: New Harbinger, 2013.

Ricci, Isolina. *The Co-Parenting Toolkit: The Essential Supplement for Mom's House, Dad's House.* La Vergne, TN: Lightning Source, 2015.

Schulman, Diana. *Co-Parenting After Divorce: How to Raise Happy, Healthy Children in Two-Home Families.* Sherman Oaks, CA: Winnspeed Press, 1996.

Wallerstein, Judith, Julia M. Lewis, and Sandra Blakeslee. *The Unexpected Legacy of Divorce.* New York: Hachette, 2001.

Tech and Media

Awareness Technologies Inc. WebWatcher website, www.webwatcher.com (*Information on monitoring software*).

Common Sense Media website, www.commonsensemedia.org (*One-stop shop for reviews on TV, movies, music, games, books, and websites—excellent resource*).

McAfee. InternetSafety website, www.internetsafety.com (*Safe Eyes Internet filter*).

National Center for Missing and Exploited Children. NetSmartz website, www.netsmartz.org (*Very popular safety site used by educators, law enforcement, and parents*).

WiredSafety website, www.wiredsafety.com (*Internet safety site*).

Parenting Styles

Cohen, Lawrence J. *The Opposite of Worry: The Playful Parenting Approach to Childhood Anxieties and Fears.* New York: Ballantine, 2013.

Miles, Karen. *The Power of Loving Discipline.* New York: Penguin, 2006.

Semmelroth, Carl. *The Anger Habit in Parenting: A New Approach to Understanding and Resolving Family Conflict.* Naperville, IL: Sourcebooks, 2005.

Stiffelman, Susan. *Parenting with Presence: Practices for Raising Conscious, Confident, Caring Kids.* Novato, CA: New World Library, 2015.

Child Temperament

Borsky, Bari. *Authentic Parenting: A Four Temperaments Guide to Understanding Your Child—And Yourself!* Herndon, VA: SteinerBooks, 2013.

Dodson, James C. *The New Strong-Willed Child.* Carol Stream, IL: Tyndale Momentum, 2014.

Other Discipline Alternatives

Farber, Adele, and Elaine Mazlish. *Siblings without Rivalry: How to Help Your Children Live Together So You Can Live Too.* New York: W. W. Norton & Company, 2012.

Leman, Kevin. *Have a New Kid by Friday! How to Change Your Child's Attitude, Behavior & Character in 5 Days.* Grand Rapids, MI: Revell, 2012.

MacKenzie, Robert J. *Setting Limits with Your Strong-Willed Child: Eliminating Conflict by Establishing Clear, Firm, and Respectful Boundaries.* New York: Three Rivers Press, 2013.

Markham, Laura. *Peaceful Parent, Happy Kids: How to Stop Yelling and Start Connecting.* New York: Perigree, 2012.

Research on 1-2-3 Magic

Allen, Sharon M., Roy H. Thompson, and Jane Drapeaux. "Successful Methods for Increasing and Improving Parent and Child Interactions." Paper Presented at the 24th Annual Training Conference of the National Head Start Association, Boston, May 25–31, 1997.

Bradley, Susan, Darryle-Anne Jadaa, Joel Brody, et al. "Brief Psychoeducational Parenting Program: An Evaluation and 1-Year Follow-Up." *Journal of the American Academy of Child and Adolescent Psychiatry* 42, no. 2 (2003): 1171–78. doi:10.1097/01.chi.0000081823.25107.75.

Elgar, Frank J., and Patrick J. McGrath. "Self-Administered Psychosocial Treatments for Children and Families." *Journal of Clinical Psychology* 59, no. 3 (2003): 321–39. doi:10.1002/jclp.10132.

Norcross, John C., Linda F. Campbell, John M. Gohol, et al. *Self-Help That Works: Resources to Improve Emotional Health and Strengthen Relationships*, 162, 165. New York: Oxford University Press, 2013.

Porzig-Drummond, Renata, Richard J. Stevenson, and Carol Stevenson. "The 1-2-3 Magic Parenting Program and Its Effect on Child Problem Behaviors and Dysfunctional Parenting: A Randomized Controlled Trial." *Behavior Research and Therapy* 58C (May 2014): 52–64. doi: 10.1016/j.brat.2014.05.004.

Tutty, Steve, Harlan Gephart, and Katie Wurzbacher. "Enhancing Behavioral and Social Skill Functioning in Children Newly Diagnosed with Attention Deficit Hyperactivity Disorder in a Pediatric Setting." *Developmental and Behavioral Pediatrics* 24, no. 1 (2003): 51–57.

Salehpour, Yeganeh. "1-2-3 Magic Part I: Its Effectiveness on Parental Function in Child Discipline with Preschool Children." Abstract. *Dissertation Abstracts International*, Section A: Humanities & Social Sciences 57, no. 3-A (Sept 1996): 1009.

ABOUT THE AUTHORS

Thomas W. Phelan, PhD, is an internationally renowned expert, author, and lecturer on child discipline and attention-deficit/hyperactivity disorder. A registered clinical psychologist, he appears frequently on radio and TV. Dr. Phelan practices and works in the western suburbs of Chicago.

Photo © Billie Jo Gwaltney
Photography

Tracy M. Lee is the family engagement specialist in the Virginia Department of Education's Office of Dispute Resolution and Administrative Services. She has also been an elementary school teacher, preschool director, and family resource coordinator for Colonial Heights Public Schools in Colonial Heights, VA. Additionally, she has appeared nationwide on ABC, CBS, NBC, and Fox affiliates, discussing parenting- and education-related issues.